STRAIGHT OUTTA LINE

Wrong Place, Wrong Time

To Ms Bradis, thanks for the support And may God bless

Garry "Goldwater" Jones

12-5-2012

Written By:

Garry Lamonte Jones

A4J Publishing
P.O. Box 1101
Orlando, FL 32802
www.a4jpublishing.com

Copyright © 2009 by Garry L. Jones

Without limiting the rights under copyright reserved above, no part of this publication may be reproduced, stored in or introduced into a retrieval system, or transmitted, in any form or by any means, without prior written permission of both the copyright owner and publisher of this book. Your support of the author's rights is appreciated.

Cover Design Concept: Garry L. Jones
Cover Design Artwork: Rholee Concepts & Designs
Editor: Vikki Marie Hankins

Manufactured in the United States of America

ISBN: 978-0-9831372-2-1

Publisher's Note:
The names and characters have been changed to protect the privacy of such individuals. Some expressions in this book are based on the author's opinions and beliefs, yet not intended to demean any race, religion or person(s); the intent is not to make anyone uncomfortable.

www.garryjones.info

This book is dedicated in the memory of Tessie Simmons Jones

SUNRISE: FEBRUARY 28, 1925   **SUNSET: JANUARY 16, 2009**

WHO WAS TESSIE JONES

Tessie Jones was a virtuous woman, the matriarch and the strength of the Jones family who had a lot of pride. She took on a tremendous responsibility when my grandfather Wesley died. She was a mother, grandmother, aunt, cousin, friend, neighbor, and was willing to help others first and set her own work to the side.

Tessie Jones was a very loving and humble woman until you crossed that line, when her family was in danger she wasn't so kind. Her love was unconditional and she was very faithful to the church, and who did you call on when others were neglecting God's work? Could that be Tessie Jones?

Tessie Jones used to cook a full course meal each and everyday; she knew her children and grandchildren needed energy in order to work and go outside to play. Tessie Jones supplied us with spiritual food as well, and while living in her house she made sure we attended Sunday School, Church, and Vacation Bible School without fail.

Tessie Jones was a strong woman and whenever sickness put her on her back, she would find the energy to make a great big comeback. No, she didn't tell us she loved us everyday, but she did express her love in a very special way. Is there anyone out there that can follow in her footsteps today?

Tessie Jones, it took me years to understand your character and unique ways. I didn't know you were laying down the foundation to help the family pave the way for others one day. Could it be because you could show me better than you could tell me and if that was the case, thanks for letting your light shine so the world could see.

Written by: Garry Lamonte Jones
www.garryjones.info

Acknowledgments

First and foremost I would like to give thanks to my Lord and Savior Jesus Christ; without him none of my work would have been possible.

I would like to give thanks to my friends and family who have supported me from the beginning - whether they be near or far.

I would like to thank the people who have prayed for me and continue to pray for me that I stay on the right path and do not lose the desire to fight for justice. I definitely would like to thank my cousin Veleria Holloway who is always saying cousin I'm praying for you all the time.

I would like to say hello to my beautiful children Derrick "Deon" Sutton, LaToya "Nicole" Jones, Malcolm "Keith-Goldwater" Jones and my daughter-in-law Sherrie Black Sutton and to my grandchildren Dereon Sutton and Jada Jones.

I would also like to give thanks to the President of the Advocate4justice organization, non other than my brother Mr. Terry G. Jones. The main thing I want to say about him is he hasn't changed. He is still a no-nonsense type of guy who knows how to budget.

I would like to give thanks to the Vice President and friend of A4J and that is Vikki Marie Hankins. She is one of the hardest working young ladies I have ever met. Don't let people fool you she is the backbone of the organization. Without her this organization would have crashed a long time ago. Her talent and skills are impeccable. She is also the Webmaster of the website www.advocate4justice.org. Go out and purchase her latest book entitled "Trauma".

I would like to give additional thanks to Vikki Marie Hankins for all of the hard work she put into Straight Out of Hell 1. She transcribed for nearly four months trying to understand the points I wanted to make; I jumped from one subject to the next and at times I was not audible on the original recordings that are over 13 years old – making it extremely difficult for her to accomplish the task. Even though this book was recorded 13 years ago, it took a full year to go to print. But the job is finally done! Thank you Vikki for all of the hard work you put into Straight Out of Hell 1, 2 & 3!

To my sister Lisa Jones, who made life hard because all of the boys wanted her - I had to fight to keep them off of her. Hang in there Sis! As long as you don't date anyone *I know*, everything will be just fine.

I give thanks to Thomas B. Jones and Lauren M. Fletcher for taking time out of their busy schedule to give constructive criticism of my book.

My brother, Duane King, and my sisters Alicia Rooks and Kayla Dove, thank you for your continued support.

I would also like to thank Maurice Van Buren Parker for interviewing me for my book.

I would like to thank my graphic design artist Miss Rhoda Williams from the great state of California, (Daly City). Rhoda is also a hard working woman whom I have called on, on many occasions – she's never let me down.

Rhoda and Terry I know I'm in your debt, but once this book takes off, I will pay you in full!!!!!!!!!!!

CHAPTER 1

Depression

It was Friday, May 24, 1996 in Tallahassee, Florida. One of my closest friends flew down from Washington, D.C. to interview me for my first book. It was a beautiful morning in Florida and he and I started collaborating on this very important project.

"Gold, can you turn on the air-conditioner?"

(Gold is one of my nicknames).

"Sure my brother, is there anything else you want me to do?"

"No, Gold, I just wanted to be relaxed when we start this project. By the way, why are you writing a book and why are you calling this book 'Straight Out of Hell?"

"Sure Parker, I can tell you how I came up with the title, but first let me get a beer and turn on some Frankie Beverly and Maze to get me relaxed. The title 'Straight Out of

Hell' came from a vision I had; that one day God would bring me out of the hell that I had been going through since I was a kid and I would live to give my testimony."

"G, I have known you all of my life and I have never seen any *hell* that you have gone through. I know that you suffered from asthma yet you still played sports and you were good at it. I also knew you had a speech impediment."

"Man, stop being politically correct by saying 'speech impediment,' you know good and damn well I used to stutter and the way Tommy Jones used to tease me when I talked. I don't know if Tommy knew it or not, but it was rather upsetting and nerve wrecking when he teased me, to say the least but I survived. There are a few things that you have seen on the *outside* but you never knew what was going on the *inside*. It's not just the asthma or the ulcers, it's the pain and suffering from major depression that I never spoke of."

"G, what do you mean when you say you have been suffering from major depression. Every time I saw you, you always had a smile on your face and you were popular in the community with your skinny ass self.

On the serious side G, I really wouldn't have known that you suffered from depression. I am sure a lot of other people didn't know either."

"Well, P, it was a secret that I didn't want to *get out*."

"So why are you telling the secret now and how have you managed to live through it?"

"I feel as if my testimony would help someone else deal with the illness."

"Brother, I'm listening, give your testimony."

"When I was about six or seven years old, I used to wake up and for some reason I would be crying silently and never knew what I was crying about. I would cry at night when everyone was asleep and sometimes I would go to the cemetery alone to shed some tears.

When I was at school, I would feel like crying, but of course, I just couldn't cry in front of everyone because I didn't want anyone to pick on me for being a cry baby."

"G, I do remember seeing you cry at school."

"Yes, you may have seen me crying but what you saw was the pain I was going through with my ulcers or not being able to breathe because of an asthma attack. Of course this gave me an excuse to cry without losing face."

"G, when you were suffering from depression, why didn't you let anyone know?"

"How in the hell could I let anyone know when I didn't know what was going on myself. I was a kid; I didn't know what mental pain was about until I got older."

"I can see you are getting angry; you always had a temper."

"The reason I'm getting angry is because you asked that dumb-ass question. You and the rest of the world don't understand how it feels to suffer on the inside because *you* are not the one's suffering. Sometimes I feel as though I'm living with a demonic spirit inside of me but I have to put on a front for everyone else. Man, do you realize, it was hard for me to concentrate in school.

I couldn't remember my plays when I played sports. I felt like committing suicide at a young age! This disease is not a joke. When I became older, I went to my family physician and told him what was going on. He told me I was suffering from depression; he wanted to send me to a shrink. I told him, I would not go see a shrink, nor would I take any pills because if I did that, people were going to think that I was crazy."

"G, let me get back to my first question. Why are you so adamant about speaking out about depression now?"

"The reason I'm talking about it now is because there are so many people committing suicide because they feel the way that I feel on the inside, they feel hopeless and see no end in sight. There is help out there for us. But we allow the public to label us as 'crazy.' Black people have got to get away from this type of attitude. If we suffer from depression, then we need to seek help; the hell with what the world thinks. If you suffer from diabetes, you take insulin; if you suffer from asthma, you receive asthma medication; if you have a toothache, you go to the dentist and so on. Why can't we go to the psychiatrist when we have a mind disease? I have suffered long enough and now it is time to educate people on this deadly disease."

"G, as a friend I really didn't know that you had suffered in silence for so long. When I think back, the only thing I can remember is that you were good in sports, popular around the neighborhood, and popular with the women. You mentioned earlier that it was hard for you to concentrate in school and sports. How did you compensate for this lack of concentration? You weren't a dumb brother, you played sports well, and you always had a smile on your face."

"Looking back P, I realized that it couldn't have been me. It was what was on the inside of me fighting the demonic spirit. It was God saving me. It was God doing for me what I couldn't do for myself. I was the clay and God was the potter and he was molding me then as I was growing up; I just didn't know it. He always had a hedge of protection around me! My family was a part of this protective equation."

CHAPTER 2

Carver Courts

Front Row Left to Right, Uncle John Jones, Grandmother Tessie Jones and Uncle Earl Jones
Second Row Left to Right, Cousin Annie Mae Grimes, Aunt Mamie Johnson, Denderant Jones, Aunt Arnetta Dixon, Mother Vergie Chalmers, Aunt Mary Mason, and Aunt Mavis Jones
(My Family)

"Let's talk about the childhood days, because you know we grew up in Carver Courts. Carver Courts was a Housing Project for low income families."

"I really don't like to say 'low income', but you are right, it was for families with low income. The reason why I don't appreciate people saying low income is because the projects where I grew up produced lawyers, doctors, musician, teachers, and a judge."

"G, these people were working on their law degree, medical degree, and music degrees; these people that you speak of, got these degrees *after* they left the projects."

"That's a lie, if that were the case why was my Uncle Jay teaching and still living in the household (the projects). Why was my Aunt Denderant a Guidance Counselor and living in our household (the projects) and why was my Uncle Hamm working at one of the top paying jobs in Kinston while living in the household. Maceo Parker lived in Carver Courts and he had just started his career in the music field *and* he started playing with James Brown. You can't say everyone who became successful did so "after" they left the projects because some people were successful while living in the projects."

"If the people were successful in their field, why were they still staying at home (the projects)?"

"I don't know but I have a pretty good idea. In my opinion one of the reasons was they were trying to help their parents out and another reason was that it wasn't easy for a black person to get a house unless they had pretty good credit and a lot of money to pay down on a house. You know just as well as I do, that most blacks could afford a mortgage, but it was the high down payment and the credit that was holding them back. Whites that were in power didn't want blacks to achieve the 'American Dream' of owning their own home. They wanted us to continue to rent."

"You said a mouth full. I must admit we had some intelligent people who came out of the projects. For instance, Mrs. Esther Belle Jones and that family of eight children she had. I know she had a hard time trying to raise six boys and two girls without a father - it was almost the same for you all when Mr. Wesley died. She produced the first black Judge in Lenoir County and a General Surgeon. That was pretty impressive along with two people working in the school system from your home. It was something that black parents did and they did well. I want to commend any family today that has achievers with one parent; it's usually a mother."

CHAPTER 3

The Bonding the Projects Created

"G, what would you say helped you the most while living in the projects?"

"It was the bond that each family had. The one thing the projects were guaranteed to produce was a bond with each family member. It's not like the projects today where you can't trust each other. The way the projects used to be back then, if your child did something wrong and another adult found out, that adult would whip your ass and when you got home and you had another ass whipping coming.

It was all about family ties. Our neighborhood was a family-oriented society. We had a community. Carver Courts and the surrounding projects like Richard Green, Simon Bright, Mitchell Wooten and Holloway Courts were communities within themselves.

As a matter of fact we didn't consider our community a project because it didn't look like the typical projects up North, the Midwest, and other Western states.

Me on the Outside of Our Home in the Projects (Carver Courts)

When they say projects you think of a high rise, poverty-stricken housing, and ghetto type places. As a matter of fact we didn't live in a high rise. We lived in what you might call townhouses or something similar. I mean, if you think about it, we had an upstairs with three to four bedrooms, downstairs with a living room and a kitchen and believe it or not, we had a pantry.

Me on the Inside of our Home in the Projects

I'm not ashamed of where I came from because if it weren't for the projects I wouldn't be the man I am today. I'm a strong family man with good old-fashioned family values. That means I knew to take care of my responsibilities and to be responsible for my actions and their consequences."

"Jones, I remember you as a snot-nosed kid who used to like to fight and couldn't beat anybody."

"I begged to differ, I've lost only one fight in my life and that was to a guy three years my senior and I truly believe that fight was a tie. Parker, you are mad because I used to whip your ass and kick the hell out of you with my cowboy boots and the reason I didn't continue whipping on your ass is because my brother Pete was a real close friend of yours.

Parker the only thing you were good at was books and being a good ole Seventh Day Adventist. You helped the guys out in the neighborhood with their homework, but you didn't help me out because my Uncle Jay and Pete helped me out."

"Was 'Jay' your uncle or brother?"

"Man, you know good and damn well Jay was my uncle and he was the man of the house. Man, you need to stop asking these questions you know the answer to."

"Matter of fact speaking of Jay, let's talk about him."

"What do you want to know?"

"What influence did he have on you?"

"My grandmother, the rest of my aunts and Jay helped raise me. Man, you know this shit, stop tripping with the questions. Growing up, I saw what was going on, my mother left to go stay in D.C. and you knew her reputation, you knew how young and wild my mother was, you knew she was out there in the streets and my father didn't spend that much time with us. So Jay, being the man that he is became the father figure."

"Jones, I know how devastating of an affect something like this could be on a kid."

"How would you know, your father and mother were both in your household. I used to hear a lot of negative things about *my* father."

"What sort of things, Jones?"

"My Aunt Denderant used to say neither my father nor my mother wanted us and that my brother and I needed to bond instead of fighting because we only had but each other.

'You all don't have anyone but each other,' were harsh words but Jay took another approach. Instead of adding fuel to the fire, he kept his comments to himself in reference to my father. Jay's attitude was, 'My sister left the children on his mother,' so he decided to help raise us to take the stress off of my grandmother.

As I got older, Jay realized that I loved sports but he wanted me to also be involved in getting a good education. He knew I could go a long way with education, but at the same time he was a *teacher* and at one time he was an All American Quarterback in college. Jay understood things had to be put in their proper perspective. He was that strong, positive, male role model that most kids are lacking today.

Jay was the first person that made me realize that in order to live in this world and be successful you had to read! He put emphasis on reading educational stuff, not just *Sports Illustrated, Jet* magazine or *Ebony*.

He wanted me to read positive things; things that were going to help me out in life; I couldn't see it back then. I didn't *want* to see it back then, because I didn't like to read. He told me to read something everyday.

I hated reading. My comprehension skills were average because I didn't read a lot. It's ironic because whenever I read something I liked, I could recite everything I had just read, but when it came to something I didn't like I couldn't recite a damn thing. It's amazing how the mind works. I remember Jay taking me with him when he went to Fayetteville, North Carolina. He was going to pick up a stereo set and while we were riding, he would point out the signs on the highway and explain to me what the signs meant, signs such as 'railroad crossing,' 'slippery when wet,' 'one way streets,' 'slow down when coming around a curve' and other highway signs.

I was about ten years old...he was teaching me about the signs on the highway, in reality he was teaching me about how important it was to know how to read.

Jay was trying to instill in me that success depended on your being able to read. I appreciate him because now I realize that he was a significant part of my life; my aunts, my grandmother and my other Uncle Hamm, played significant roles in the overall success of my life as well."

CHAPTER 4

Big Bad Denderant Jones

My Aunt Denderant Jones was a complete hell-raiser, a no-nonsense type of woman. She was the type of aunt that loved you but wouldn't show it. It was hard to comprehend her love. If you looked at her wrong she would fuss you out and she's still that way today. Everyone in the projects knew she didn't play. I guess her love was tough love, but her love damn near drove me crazy.

She would give me money or buy me things and when I would ask her a question she would go to fussing. I guess the pressure was getting to her as well, having to raise her nephews and nieces. I love my mother even though she wasn't there, but my mother's lack of raising us put a lot of pressure on her siblings.

My aunts and uncles had to give up a lot of things because food and clothes had to go towards feeding the nephews and nieces. Not only did my grandmother make sure that we got everything we needed, but my uncles and aunts played a major role in giving us things that my grandmother couldn't give. My grandmother's oldest children Mamie (Jean), Arnetta, and Mary, were staying up north and they contributed as well.

I came to realize why my Aunt Denderant was a no-nonsense type of woman. Denderant became irritated because it was her sister that was out there having these babies not her. My mother was gone and expected my grandmother to raise these babies.

Denderant was one of those aunts that you had to grow to love. She treated my friends like shit, whenever I would have company, she would tell them, "Take your stinky tails home and don't come back."

Denderant was the type of person when she tell you to do something you better do it, I don't give a damn if you are sleep, doing cartwheels, flips or whatever; if you didn't do your chores around the house, she would come on the basketball court in front of your friends and embarrass the hell out of you.

I remember one time we were on the basketball court playing an official game, I think it was Carver Courts against Richard Green, we were playing a serious game and Josh Wooten was refereeing the game; they had tables out on the basketball courts, and people keeping the score. You know that was the thing around summer time, playing basketball.

Denderant came out there, "You bring your butt home right now, I said bring your butt home right now and empty this trash."

This shit was embarrassing, even the fellows were afraid of her. When my cousins Ross Johnson, Curtis Johnson, Cedric Dixon, Garrick Dixon and my cousin Sharon Mason came from up north, they would fall up under Dender's raft. What Dender said went, no questions asked.

Dender's other sister Mavis (Colleen), took a different approach, she wasn't mean like Denderant, but if you left the house without being well-groomed, she would come and get you then comb your hair and make sure you didn't go back outside until you looked decent.

My mother had four children by the age of eighteen; Me, Pete, Lisa, and Jr. and we were all raised in the same household. My brother Jr. would later go stay with his father in Texas. When my sister Lisa was in the 9th grade she got out of hand and she would later leave North Carolina and go stay with my mother in Washington, D.C., even though her stay was short. After one year with my mother, Lisa would join her brother Jr. in Texas.

I must admit, when I got older, I didn't realize that my grandmother's two youngest children weren't that much older than me and my brother Pete.

Today, Denderant still is a no-nonsense woman but she gives us anything that we want; she even helps me out with my kids as well, so does my Aunt Mavis.

Later on in life my Aunt Dender had a son of her own. His name was Larry Burney Jr. (L.B., L-Mak, The Bisel to the Diesel). L.B. is her pride and joy and after having him life became easy for everyone but for only a short period of time. Therefore, I am grateful and appreciative that my Grandmother

had that much love for her daughter (my mother), that she kept us and gave us a great life.

CHAPTER 5

My Mother's Troubled Past

"G, you mentioned your mother earlier, but you never went into details about her."

"It's hard to go in to details about my mother. Like I said earlier she had my brother Pete at the age of fourteen, she had me at the age of fifteen, she had my sister Lisa at the age sixteen and she had my brother Leslie aka Jr. at the age of seventeen. If I'm not mistaken my mother had all of her kids in Carver Courts with the exception of my brother Jr.

What I'm trying to say is she had all of her kids early. She was a young mother and she didn't take care of us; our grandmother, aunts and uncles took on this responsibility. I don't hold this against her because we had everything we needed as kids but there were times that I used to wonder what type of kid would I have been if I was raised by my mother.

My Birth Certificate – I Was Born in a Backroom

    My mama dropped out of high school probably at the age of sixteen - I think at the time a person couldn't drop of out of school unless they were sixteen years old.

    She got married to this dude named Nick, which is Jr.'s father. Nick was stationed at Camp Lejeune in Jacksonville, North Carolina. She never married my father, she married Nick. She met him in Kinston. Our home town Kinston is where a lot of marines used to come and pick up women. I guess Nick swept her off her feet and they got married.

After they got married she moved on base with him. My siblings and I used to go on base and stay for a little while but my grandfather found out there were some fighting in front of us, so he didn't allow us to go back on base. He didn't want his grandchildren to witness the violent relationship my mother and Nick had. The only thing I can remember about Camp Lejeune was that my brother and I had our tonsils taken out.

Before my grandfather died, he made my grandmother make a promise to him on his death bed. This was in the year of 1970. He told my grandmother to make sure she raised me and my brother Pete. He also told her that she was probably going to have trouble out of my sister Lisa, but do not let the grand boys get out of her site.

My grandmother fulfilled my grandfather's dream. My grandmother was a strong black woman even though she was high yellow damn near looking white, but I loved the hell out of her. I was going through some photos and seen my great grandmother; I didn't know she was an Indian and my great grandfather was very dark-skinned.

When my grandmother told you to do something she meant it and this lady would fuss all the time. I think this is where Denderant got all of her fussing from. My grandmother would always talk about how she was raised, even though she was the youngest of nine children, she would often talk about how they lived on a farm and she was just as strong as her older sisters and brothers.

When she would talk about this she would always have a smile on her face. I believed my grandmother when she said she was just as strong as her brothers and sisters because whenever we got in trouble, my grandmother would knock you to summerset. Summerset was a place unknown and unheard of.

My grandmother was the type of woman who loved her grandchildren. She allowed us to make some mistakes and she encouraged us to be ourselves, but when our behavior got out of hand and we started talking back, she would hit us with a backhand and we'd land on the floor. We could get away with almost anything except talking back and she made sure we address her as 'Yes ma'am.'

As we got older and the children got out of hand, that's when my Uncle Jay would instill the discipline. Can you imagine going to school where your uncle was the teacher and at home he was the disciplinarian. My siblings and I couldn't act up in school because the teachers knew Jay was our uncle and as soon as we got in trouble we would be sent to Jay's room only to get a paddling in the hallway. It didn't stop there; we got our asses tore out the frame when we got home.

My grandmother knew if I got into trouble in school, someone had to provoke me, so she didn't just take that person's side. The teachers used to send my report card home with an unsatisfactory note in there about my conduct. My grandmother didn't believe everything that a teacher said about her grandchildren, especially me. If the teachers wrote a note about my sister Lisa conduct she was more likely to believe the teacher; it was very rare that my brother Pete got bad conduct. Pete was slick, he never showed his trump card. If you said anything about Pete, my grandmother would turn a deaf ear.

I can remember one incident about my brother that shocked my grandmother. It was during Christmas time; my grandmother used to always have some homemade wine that she had gotten from someone in the country. The wine always stayed in the closet. This particular night Pete was going in the kitchen closet from the living room but he would always exit through the kitchen door instead of coming back through the living room. He did this about three times.

Grandmother got up to see why Pete kept coming into the kitchen. She looked in the closet and realized the wine she had in the closet was getting low. Of course my grandmother didn't drink.

My grandmother got suspicious and went through the kitchen door to the outside of the house and that's when she seen my brother with a jar with wine in it. Pete was stealing the wine and giving it to Shellcat and the boys.

My grandmother was shocked because she never would have thought Pete would be stealing, or should I say taking the wine and giving it away. This type of behavior was expected of me but not Pete. I didn't drink at all; as a matter of fact I didn't drink my first beer until I graduated from high school. My brother Pete doesn't drink alcohol at all.

My grandmother would allow my aunts and uncle to discipline us but she didn't allow them to go too far. If she felt like the punishment didn't fit the action taken by my uncles and aunt, my grandmother would overturn their punishment and drop it down to a lesser punishment. What I'm trying to say is, if we were getting ready to get corporal punishment for something minor, my grandmother would step in and say, "No whipping today, the children just won't go outside to play."

She tried not to ever overrule Denderant or Jay; she knew they were trying to raise us to do the right thing and in that sense she never overruled them.

She took care of me and spoiled me, because I was a real sick growing up. I had ulcers and asthma and the secret disease called depression. I was this pitiful little boy.

CHAPTER 6

How Doctors Treated Black and White Kids

When I used to have asthma attacks, the doctors would prescribe this bad tasting medication that made me vomit. They didn't give black children samples of the *new* medications. When they prescribed medication for the black kids to take; if it didn't work they would write another prescription and if the second prescription didn't work, you'd go back and got a shot in your arm. My grandmother wasn't making much money and all her money went towards my medication.

Sometimes I felt like a burden to the family because I was sick a lot and most of the time, my grandmother would have to take off work to take me to the doctor. It wasn't until I got older that I realized white doctors treated white children different than black children when it came to medical care.

When my daughter was born, she was born with asthma. I remember the first time she had an asthma attack - I took her to the hospital, a black doctor treated her by giving her a nebulizer and a mask to breathe in the medication. This is where you put some liquid medication into the machine and breathe in the medication as not to cause you to vomit.

I told the doctor, "This must be some new technology?"

"No, these machines have been out every since the 60's."

I thought to myself, I was born in 1964 and when I was small I stayed in the doctors office taking that bullshit medication and buying Primatene mist off the counter, why didn't the doctor prescribe me a nebulizer knowing that I had a weak stomach and why didn't they prescribe me inhalers to prevent me from having asthma attacks. I remember being in school and seeing white children with inhalers but the inhalers weren't Primatene mist.

These thoughts didn't come to my mind until I took my daughter to the hospital. All of those years I suffered and the doctors didn't provide me with the best medical care. Whether my grandmother could have afforded it or not, she wasn't given the option.

The medication they gave me took two to three hours to take affect but the white children had the opportunity to feel good *right away* due to the fact they were given the best medical care. Whenever I go to the doctors now and they write me a prescription, I ask them to give me a sample - if the sample medication works, only then will I get the prescription filled.

These companies give the doctors samples to promote their medication and the doctors give them to the rich people who can afford their medication and say the hell with the poor people. They don't offer them samples.

Things have improved now, but in order for things to have a greater improvement, you have to demand that things improve by opening up your mouth and asking questions.

I know there is no cure for asthma, but if you receive good medical care for your asthma, you will feel a lot better. As much money as my grandmother spent on medication for me, she could have moved out of the projects years before she actually moved.

I remember being in the doctors office one day waiting for them to call me in for my appointment. I picked up a magazine and started to read an article about prescriptions. I read that the pharmaceutical companies send doctors and their families on paid vacation if they write a lot of prescriptions to their patients and get the prescription filled at certain pharmacies.

If you lived in a small town with only one or two drug stores, you didn't have a choice but to get your prescription filled there. The doctors and the pharmaceutical company's work hand in hand, meaning, 'If you send me business, I will send your family on a paid vacation.'

CHAPTER 7

Hustler and Sex in the Hood

In every project there is always going to be hustlers and the number rackets going on - Carver Courts was no different. My best friend's mother used to run the numbers; they call it playing the lotto these days. As a matter of fact she wasn't the only one running numbers, I can name at least eight people in the projects that I know that ran the numbers but I'm not going to name them because they might be still doing it.

Everyone played the numbers, even the people who were supposed to 'serve and protect' (the policeman). I used to love going to my best friend house because his mother played a card game call spades and she was good at it. She was a multi-tasked woman, meaning she could do a lot of things at one time.

She would play spades while holding one of her infants in one arm; deal the cards with her free hand and smoke a cigarette all at the same time. When her infant child would start crying she would take out her breast and start feeding her. That was the first time that I would consider being exposed to a breast.

While she was still playing spades, people would come over to the house and put their numbers in, she would give them a receipt and let them know she was playing cards, then turn around and tell the people that was playing spades, "It's your turn to deal the cards." She did all of this without missing a beat.

Anytime you play spades with Bonnie, you better know how to play because if you didn't you were going to get scolded, she and Josh Wooten was the only ones that would scold you if you didn't know how to play. They took the game of spade seriously. Mind you, I was nine or ten years old playing spades with adults but Josh and Bonnie didn't give a damn, they looked at you as an adult if you were their spade partner.

I reneged a couple of times when I played spades. Renege means to go back on one's word or promise but when you renege in playing cards it means to play a card that is not of the same suit led when one can follow suit.

For example for the people who do not know anything about spades…if the other team played a club, and you played a spade card to cut the team hand (book) to win and later on during the game when the other team played a club and then you played a club, that is called 'reneging' and once the other team discovered that you reneged, they are obligated to take three of your books that you had won.

The taking of the three books can cause the other team to be set and lose the game. Take for another example if a team said that they could win five books and they made their five books but the other team discovered you reneged; they would take three of your books which would only leave you with two books at the end of the game then you lose points.

Bonnie would say after you made a mistake, "You shouldn't have sat your ass at the table if you didn't know how to play spades." She would then make you get up from the table to replace you with a much experienced spade player.

Josh would start to stuttering when trying to explain to you how you messed up while smoking his pipe and blowing smoke in your face all at the same time. The other fellows would laugh at you.

Living in the hood you got schooled very fast. Later on Mr. Parrot would come around and collect his money. Mr. Parrot was the gangster that lived above the café or the block - the old school people called it 'Harlem's Inn.'

This place was an eatery ran by Mr. Fuller at the time. You could tell Mr. Parrot was a gangster, he used to dress with his suit, shirt, tie, and shoes all matching. A lot of women used to come out of Mr. Parrot's apartment. I think they were his prostitutes giving him his money. After Mr. Parrot received his money, he gave my best friend's mother her cut. She would then smile and ask, "Do anyone want to play Pokeno?"

This was a game that was played for money. Several cups were put on the table, labeled as corners, center, diagonal, four of a kind, and Pokeno. Before the game started, everyone who played had to put money in each one of those cups, some people who were low on money often cheated until they were caught. It was rare that anyone could get over on my best friend's mother. She had an eye like an eagle.

This game was played with cards and whenever the right card landed your way, you could claim one of the cups with money in them, but the game stops, when someone says "Pokeno" meaning they won. Of course my best friend's mother would get her cut because the game was being played at her house.

Whenever the guys wanted to watch X-rated movies, an older friend of mine would show them at his house but you had to pay ten cents to come in. Whenever his mother would leave to go to work in the summertime, he would invite the boys over. This guy was about five years older than I was but my Aunt Denderant and his sister were pretty good friends. Denderant didn't know this was going on, but anyway this guy would show the X-rated pictures with one of the old library projectors, the machine where you had to put the film inside of this gadget and turn it on to view the picture. He didn't have the screen to show the pictures on so he just used the wall in the pantry to view the film. I used to get an eye full. If anyone in my family had any clue that this was going on, I would still be on punishment today. I would have gotten a whipping first, then placed on punishment.

Needless to say, this man went into the military. It is my understanding that he is retired; I know he is a preacher because he came from overseas to preach at home when I was growing up.

There were also some perverts in the hood. When I was playing in the recreational center, this older real bright skinned Vietnamese guy touched my sister on the butt, Lisa couldn't have been no more that ten years old. I ran out of the center to tell my Uncle Jay. Jay was a teacher at the time and normally Jay is laid back, he always quelled volatile situations but this time Jay made all the kids get out of the center.

What happened next is what surprised me. Jay moved all the ping pong tables, pool tables and chairs to the corner of the room and challenged the Vietnamese guy to come in the center of the room because he was going to give this guy a good ole Carver Courts ass whipping for touching his niece on the butt.

Jay balled up his fist - his eyes were red as fire. All the kids that Jay made leave the center, climbed on the window of the center just to see the big fight. They were all disappointed because the Vietnamese guy refused to fight Jay. It was good that Jay didn't fight the guy because Jay was a school teacher; maybe the reason why he didn't push the issue was because he could see the kids looking through the window.

Jay was a role model and this would have set a bad example for a teacher to be fighting but he had every right to whip that guy's ass. It bothers me when I hear about children being touched inappropriately by an adult. I think about what that Vietnamese did to my sister. I always taught my children that if an adult touches them in their private area to make sure they come home and tell me. I would have whipped the guy ass myself but Jay made me leave the center as well.

CHAPTER 8

Gangs In Carver Court

In the early 1970's we had gangs in Carver Courts but the purpose of the gangs were to look after the community. We didn't go around shooting and stabbing people and doing any and all type of drive-bys. We fought with our hands.

In my studies I came to understand the purpose of gangs were to protect the community by making sure no one came into the neighborhood to destroy it. The gangs that exist today are totally different. They are cowards! Destroying the property and taking human lives in your neighborhood is down right foolish to say the least it is stupid. If you have to kill someone in order to be accepted in a gang then you don't need that gang. Breaking the law is not cool and if you think so, your mind is distorted. You are committing genocide of your own race.

We created a gang in Carver Courts called the Dog Team. We marched around the whole neighborhood calling cadence D-O-G-T-E-A-M Dogteam. The entire neighborhood would stand outside and be in awe of us. We were in tuned with who we were; we didn't need anyone to tell us who we were. We were apart of something good; we motivated ourselves.

My Uncle Steve Mason came down from Washington D.C. to reside and opened up a convenient store called 'Steve's Grocery.' Steve was married to my Aunt Mary. Uncle Steve was what some people might call radical. I think he may have marched back in the 60's with the Black Panthers because I saw a photo of him with Angela Davis. Most people use radical in a negative connotation but radical is a person who advocates fundamental political, economic, and social reforms by direct and often uncompromising methods. In other words he fought for what he believed in.

He created an organization called 'Steve's Army.' If we wanted to join he ordered us military uniforms and taught us about respecting one another as well as our neighbors.

We started off as officers and then if we did something good we were promoted to corporal, sergeant, captain, and general. We had to keep our grades up in order to be in Steve's Army. Jessie Lee, Charlie Jr. and Charlie were Steve's top commanders. We had to be well-groomed and know how to march in unison.

I remember when I got my first set of green fatigues with my black army boots and I had to salute and stand in attention. This was a good feeling. We were disciplined young men. The highest rank I got was a general. Steve also taught me how to box.

Steve used to wear his Dashiki, he was pro black but this doesn't mean that he was anti-white. I also had another uncle that was pro-military and that was my Uncle Victor Johnson, he taught me a lot as well. Vick was cool and he married my Aunt Mamie (Jean).

I would be lying if I said there weren't any fights in Carver Courts because there were. Two of my friends, Albert and Ike got into arguments over playing cards or shooting pool;

I can't exactly remember which one they fought over but I do remember Albert body slamming Ike on the ground.

"Don't be there when I come back!" This is what Ike told Albert when he got up off the ground.

Albert didn't run from anyone but everyone knew if Ike said he was coming back then more than likely Ike was coming back with *something in his hands*.

A few minutes later Ike came back; he and Albert started fighting again. Ike took out a butcher knife and stabbed Albert in the chest. Albert started running away from Ike because Ike kept swinging the knife but the more Albert ran the weaker he became; Ike was running behind him trying to keep stabbing him.

If it wasn't for Tommy Jones catching up with Ike and grabbing him, Ike probably would have stabbed Albert again. When Albert got home, the ambulance was called and Albert was rushed to the hospital. Albert almost died because the stab wound was an inch away from his heart.

From time to time one would hear about someone being killed in Carver Courts, but it is nothing like the killings that goes on today in the projects.

One morning I woke up only to find out that someone was killed in my neighborhood, not with a gun but with a bat; two guys were fighting, one guy picked up a bat and hit the other guy in the head. His brains were in his ball cap he was wearing. This happened two feet away in my yard. Things like this happened far and in between. It was rare that you heard about something like this but today, it's rare if you *don't* hear of something of this nature taking place in the hood.

My best friend sister Cynthia Dixon (Cymp Juan) was fighting a guy in Carver Courts (by the way we were 'puppy lovers'). The guy that was younger than her cut her in the face because he couldn't fight like a man. He wanted to go for bad but he couldn't fight unless he had a weapon. He cut her with one of those knives called a hawk knife and he was only eleven years old. Why would a person so young carry a hawk knife?

I must say Cynthia was beating the hell out of the guy and he was embarrassed. If I'm not mistaken he went home to get the knife. She was a tough cookie, she always held her own and today she is still holding her own.

All of Mrs. Christine children held their own but when her children got in trouble, she would whip them with one of those orange racing rod tracks, she was a strict disciplinarian - all of the mother's in Carver Courts that I knew were strict disciplinarian.

Mothers like Mrs. Sue, Mrs. Willie Jay, Mrs. Dot Smith, Mrs. Esther Bell, Mrs. Neat Parker, Mrs. Hilda Williams, Mrs. Mattie Jacobs, Mrs. Swannie Irving and the list goes on.

CHAPTER 9

Joining First Baptist Church

First Baptist Church was located across the street from Carver Courts. Most of the people who stayed in Carver Courts would attend this church. From the time I was about seven years old, my siblings and I started attending First Baptist. My grandmother would always take us to her church out in the country called King's Chapel Church. I can't recall why we stopped going out in the country to attend church but whatever the reason I wasn't disappointed (my grandmother continued on going to the church in the country.)

Initially I wasn't happy about going to church but when me and my siblings attended church we had fun. I remember my first Sunday School teacher, her name was Mrs. Bannerman; I think the reason we attended her class is because of the age difference. After leaving Mrs. Bannerman's class I started attending Mrs. Burney's class. She was a lot older but she was very, very, nice. Mrs. Burney always had snacks for us when we attended her class. We would always cut-up in Mrs. Burney's class but for some reason she regained control of her class very quick by asking to read scriptures from the Sunday School books.

Another reason why I think I liked attending Mrs. Burney's class is because her class was upstairs near the balcony. We always had a contest in church or Sunday School. It was about competition and I loved competition. Mrs. Burney's class would either win the banner of attendance or the banner of offering. We always wanted to *out do* the other classes.

I think Mrs. Bannerman son was the superintendent of Sunday School and my brother Pete or my best friend Antray was the Assistant superintendent. Whenever our class would win a banner it would be announced and we had to stand up and be recognized. After Sunday School we then had to attend church, church wasn't fun at all.

The only thing fun about church was when the Holy Ghost would get into some of the members in church and they would start running all over the church shouting. My friends and I would look at each other and bust out laughing. Of course we didn't understand what was going on. We were just kids. As a matter of fact I thought First Baptist was my church home because I attended the church and I thought I was paying my tithes when I put a dime in the church offering plate when it went around.

I didn't have a clue that in order for you to belong to a church, you had to first join the church. I could never figure out why some people were putting money in the envelope instead of just dropping their money in the plate as it was passed around. This was confusing to me.

My play sister Francis Irving and I had a conversation about this.

"Gold, you are not a member of the church," she stated.

"First Baptist *is* my church!" I said with confusion.

"You are still not a *member*," she said.

Of course back then I didn't know what a *member* was. I always felt if I attended a church then that was my church.

Me Standing in Front of the 'Old' First Baptist Church
(A Portion of Church is Seen in Background)

"No, Gold you have to *join* the church" and then she went on to explain to me, "after the pastor preaches his sermon, he makes an announcement for everyone who has a desire to be a part of First Baptist Church family to come up front and do whatever the churches do to make you a member."

When I got older and started to learn more about the church; that's when I decided to make my move to join.

One Sunday Fran asked me, "Are you going to join the church?"

"Yes, but I don't want to be saved."

"You don't have to be saved just because you joined."

"Well, why is it when the people walk down the aisle the pastor save them?"

She said, "Look boy! They give you an opportunity to be a member of the church or to give your life to Christ, it's your choice."

"I still don't want to be saved, I want to wait until I get older to be saved, that's what old people do; they are the saved people."

I remember it like it was yesterday, Reverend Raynor, the pastor of First Baptist Church had just finished giving his sermon and he made that famous announcement, "If you would like to join the church come up front." Of course when you go up front, they have a chair waiting for you to sit in. The questions the pastor usually asks are, 'Do you want to join the church or do you want to give your life to Christ.'

He used to say, "While the blood is still running warm in your vein, you still have a chance to give your life to Christ."

I told the people who surrounded me that I wanted to join church but I didn't want to *give my life to Christ.* After I joined the church, all the members of the church came around and gave me the 'right handed fellowship', to this day I don't have a clue of what the 'right handed fellowship' was all about. I just knew everyone shook my hand. I can't recall whether they shook my left or right hand. The pastor announced that baptism would be the next week.

When the next week came, my grandmother took me to church on a Saturday to be baptized. I was nervous and I just wanted to get it over with. I was told to go in the back with the deacons of the church to change clothes. I was nervous about that as well, I didn't need anyone to come with me to change clothes, I was sixteen years old, I knew how to take my clothes off.

After coming from the back of the church to the front, Reverend Raynor was already in the pool of water, he motioned for me to come in the water. I hesitated and looked at my grandmother; of course she didn't show any emotions. When I stepped in the pool of water, the pastor did what pastors do and prayed; before I knew it, my head was under the water so fast that I panicked when the pastor brought me up. I was coughing and trying to get the water out of my eyes. What struck me the most was when he said, "All of your sins were washed away and now you are a child of God." These weren't his exact words but I knew what he meant.

I got out of the pool and went to the back of the church to dry off. I changed clothes and went over to my grandmother and told her that he saved me and I didn't want to be saved until I got old. This was supposed to be a baptism; he wasn't supposed to make me born again. My grandmother looked at me and said, "Let's go."

I guess her mindset was, 'This boy doesn't have a clue about anything of the church.' When I became older I realized that you can be in the church but this doesn't mean you know anything about the church. I always pride myself in not getting caught up in the 'politics' of the church.

What I mean about this is, so many people want to get close to the pastor, and they want to be buddy-buddy with the pastor as if they are trying to gain some brownie points. I never understood this until this day. What I do know is that in order to go further in your spiritual life, you must study the word, participate in bible studies and go to church. This doesn't mean that you have to be at the church before the church doors open.

If you have a family, there must be a balance. You can't neglect your family or your duties at home, whether you are a male or female spouse, because of all your time is being spent at the church.

CHAPTER 10

Carver Courts Christmas

**First Row Sister Lisa, Brother Leslie, and, of Course Me
Second Row Cousin Annie Mae Grimes, and Brother Pete
During Christmas**

I loved Christmas time in Carver Courts, like I said earlier, we were a tight knit community and during Christmas time we were even tighter. I could always feel the Christmas spirit. It was a wonderful feeling.

Our family was popular in Carver Courts and we always had a lot of company over to the house. My friends used to come over and say, "Man how did you all get so many presents under that tree." The presents we had under the tree came almost to the top of the tree; that's how many presents we had. My brother and I had at least fifteen presents a piece. Whatever we wanted for Christmas we would get.

Our aunts and uncles would ask what we wanted for Christmas and we would tell them and they would say, "You all can't get that stuff for Christmas, you all want too much."

My Aunt Denderant would say, "You all are not going to get but three things for Christmas, who do you all think you are, people don't have that type of money to get you all of that stuff, you better go get a job."

Denderant knew good damn well we weren't old enough to work. My Aunt Mavis (Colleen) would always play her 45 records and the Christmas record she played the most was, "*Please Come Home for Christmas*," by Charles Brown.

My cousin Rena Mae loved listening to this sad Christmas song called, *"What Do the Lonely Do For Christmas,"* by The Emotions. I never went without getting my grandmother a gift; I would sell some bottles and go down to Rayners Supermarket and buy her four kitchen glasses that cost a $1. I was never to be out done.

I would get my cousin Annie Mae to wrap my grandmother's gift because if it was up to me I would have just presented her gift to her on Christmas without any wrapping paper. Annie Mae would always say, "You didn't take the price tag off." None of that mattered to me.

"You know you have to go to bed early because Santa Clause and his reindeers are not going to stop by the house until you go to sleep. But you can go outside and look in the sky and see his reindeers," is what my Aunt Mavis and Aunt Denderant used to say.

For some strange reason I never seen Santa clause riding with his reindeers and I would go back in the house and tell my aunts and they would say, "You must have just missed him because we seen him earlier. Gone upstairs and go to sleep because he is not coming by until you go to sleep."

The next day when Pete, my sister Lisa, and me came down stairs, we tore through our presents looking to see what we had gotten. The very thing Denderant said we weren't going to get, we got those things plus more. We had it going on. Our Aunt Arnetta, Mamie, and Mary would always send their presents from up north. Pete and I were the first kids that had an Air Hockey - Air Hockey was expensive.

We all had bikes and some kids in the neighborhood only got a bike for Christmas but we had fifteen times the amount of gifts than anyone else. I loved my Rocking Socking Robot and all the kids would come over to play at our house until it got real late.

Denderant would say, "You need to take your stinky tails home now and play with your own toys."

None of my friends got mad at Denderant because they knew she talked like that. My Uncle Jay and Larry would stay up all night putting most of our toys together and I guess my father came over in the middle of the night to bring his presents. We got bikes every year; I think my mother Vergie, supplied us with bikes one of those years, she was living up north as well. All the kids loved to skate; we were the first ones to have the roller derby skates. I remember the year before when Annie Mae got her skates. She had the old kind where you had to put the skates together and lock it with a key.

Pete, Lisa and me and Annie Mae had a bunch of gifts. Annie Mae was older than we were so she got the *old people* toys. One year for Christmas Annie Mae got a doll baby damn near four feet tall. That doll baby was ugly as hell. My grandmother would always say, "Did you all open up my gifts that I got for ya'll?"

We kind of knew what her gifts were, it was either a pair of socks, hat, neckties, peppermint candy, gloves, or some of those orange slices candy. Every now and then my grandmother would give us some under garments. As I think about it now, my grandmother didn't have to buy us anything because our aunts and uncles bought mostly everything. Sometimes my brother and I would have Christmas cards with money in them. We had money *and* toys we were rich!!!!!!!!!!!!!!!! You couldn't tell us anything. We had the best of the best.

My cousin Rena Mae always came over and said her dream was to see a 'White Christmas.' One year she got her wish because when we were awakened for Christmas, snow was on the ground. I wished I could get those Carver Courts Christmas days back; when we moved out of Carver Courts, Christmas was never the same.

CHAPTER 11

Meeting My Father for the First Time

One evening while playing in the yard in Carver Courts a strange man came over to my grandmother's place, he was looking at me kind of strange and I didn't know who he was. I think either my Aunt Denderant or my Aunt Mavis was home at the time, they were sitting on the porch. I looked at them and they said, "That is your father."

I think maybe my father was coming back from Vietnam; finally paying us a visit. I think I was six or seven years old, I really don't know. I think this man brought a bike to the house. It was strange when they said, 'This is your father,' because to me *my father* was already dead.

My grandfather died May 19, 1970 and he was the only *father* I ever knew, as a matter of fact we called my grandfather, father. Anyway this guy with this mustache came over to speak to me and I really didn't know what to say. He knew me but I didn't know him. I think I asked him his name, I can't recall what he said.

Anyway his name was Milton Dove Jr., but as the future predicted, he has never been called by this name. The only person that called him Milton Dove was my grandfather that is living, and my grandfather's name is Milton Dove Sr. My father and grandfather have an auto shop together called, *Dove and Son's Garage.*

My grandfather would often call him Milton Jr. but everyone in Kinston would call him his famous nickname, "Meat Dove." How and why he got this name I will never know.

Getting back to how we met, everything was silent with my aunts, you couldn't hear a word. They were staring at my reaction and my reaction was just like any kid who meets a stranger. I felt very uncomfortable. I can't recall our conversation but I'm quite sure it was short because I didn't know what to say. Maybe my aunts were quiet because I really looked like the guy and maybe it was confirmed that I was his child by the looks.

My Father, 'Meat Dove' When He Was Younger

A Photo of Me, When I Was Near His Age in the Above Photo

It was rumored that my father denied my brother as his child. If that was the case, my aunts were probably saying to themselves, 'There is no way he can deny him.'

Shortly after talking with my father, he went on about his business.

I remember my father coming to my grandmother's apartment again. He asked my grandmother could he take me for a ride, I can't recall what kind of car he had but I know the car was green. He took me to McDonalds and bought me a cheeseburger and some fries. For some strange reason, he asked me how my asthma was doing, I couldn't figure out how he knew about me having asthma; I'm sure my mother Vergie told him this because she usually tells him everything - I found this out later on that my mother told my father everything about his kids.

While I was eating and talking with my father, all of a sudden he asked me a strange question. He asked me was I afraid of dying because of my asthma? I don't remember what I said, but I did find out that he had asthma. My Aunt Denderant used to say something similar to this.

Whenever I would have an asthma attack, she would say with her fast talking self, "Boy, are you going to die!!!!!!!? Because you need to let somebody know."

Man, my Aunt Denderant would say some wild shit. After I finished eating my father took me back home. He wouldn't come around that much but I do remember when he came around and picked me up on his motor cycle.

He took me riding down Queen Street; riding about one hundred miles per hour! That was the last time I would ever ride on his motorcycle. I realized this man was crazy!

When I found out where my father's shop was located I would often go over there and ask him for some money. As a matter of fact I could see my father's shop from Carver Courts. I found out very fast how stingy my father was.

"The only way you can get some money from me is you work for it," he made this very clear.

When I asked my father for fifty cents, he would tell me to go get the broom and sweep the garage, not only did he mean that, he would always ask me a thousand questions, 'What do you need the money for, when do you need it?'

I didn't care about how many questions he asked, the only thing I cared about was getting the fifty cents. My brother would do the same thing, he would go over to the shop and ask my father for some money and he would ask him a thousand questions as well. My brother didn't have the patience that I had; my brother is not going to beg you for a damn thing.

Anyway when Pete did ask my father for some money, my father told him to go get in his truck. Naturally my brother did as he was told. My father drove him to the Kinston Daily Free Press and immediately got him a job as a paperboy. I don't know how long my brother kept the job, but he didn't ask my father for anymore money and he didn't go back to the shop. I was the one that kept going back to the shop asking for money.

When I was about eleven years old, my father would come by my grandmother's apartment and take us to get some school clothes.

Even though my father was stingy as hell, he would take us to the most expensive stores in Kinston, stores like H. Stadium and Brody's. They had good quality clothes but I would later find out why my father took us to these expensive clothing stores. He took us to these stores because when you buy clothes from them, you didn't have to worry about those clothes wearing out as easily because of the material that it was made from, it wasn't cheap. This meant my father didn't have to buy us clothes as often.

Still when I was around my father, the conversation was short because I didn't know what to say. When my brother and I would go to his family reunion, his family would stare at us especially his sisters. This was uncomfortable because I only knew my father's youngest sister Lorna. She and I was only a year apart. I didn't know my father's oldest sisters Velma, Timber, and Kaye. I hadn't been around my father's family that much. I would hear his sisters saying, "He look just like Bunky." My father's sister called him by another one of his nicknames.

My brother and I would get in a corner to ourselves and wouldn't say anything. It appears everyone knew each other but we didn't know them. The only people me and my brother knew was the workers at my father's shop and we spoke with them. My brother and I were ready to go home.

As I said earlier, my father was stingy and whenever he could find a way to save some money he would. My father had built us a Go Cart and came to my grandmother's house, we had just recently moved out of the projects; he asked my grandmother if he could take us riding on the Go Cart.

It was on a Saturday afternoon. He took us to the Kinston Shirt factory parking lot; the people that worked there didn't work on Saturdays and their parking lot was big but empty. When we got out of my fathers truck, he asked who wanted to ride first and of course I said I did. He showed me were the gas and brake pedals were. He cranked up the Go Cart and I went to driving that thing like I was at a NASCAR racing competition.

My brother didn't want to ride the Go Cart but my father made him ride it anyway. While my brother was riding the Go Cart either the brakes went out or he panicked because he ran the Go Cart up under another car and messed up his legs. My brother hated my father for that and until today, he still resents my father for making him ride it.

When we went back home my grandmother was furious. She didn't care that much for my father but she never said that around us, but you could see it in her eyes. My brother and father's relationship grew further apart and today they still don't have a relationship. This wasn't because of the Go Cart incident it was because my brother never cared for our father.

I think it was because my brother may have found out the rumor of my father denying him was true. It is enough to be denied, but to whole a grudge for this long is something else. *I'm the one that is notorious for holding grudges not my brother*. I never asked my father did he deny my brother and I never asked my brother, why he doesn't like our father? To tell you the truth, I really can't say my brother is holding a grudge against my father, he just don't associate himself with my father. He was my biological father but my grandfather, Mr. Wesley Jones was *my father*, until the day he died; my Uncle Jay and Hamm took up the slack and were dads for us before they had their own blood children.

CHAPTER 12

The KKK

When I was growing up, I used to be a batboy for the baseball team my Uncle Jay played for. I think the name of the team was called, 'Dapp's Party Store.' When they would go to Smithfield, North Carolina - known as KKK country – most of the team would have to put guns in the trunk of the car because the people in Smithfield were known to start shit with black people.

When the team arrived in Smithfield to play ball, we could see the rednecks ready to start trouble as soon as we hit the field. The umpire (who was from Smithfield) would make as many bad calls against our team as he could. You had to be perfect just to beat the team in Smithfield. You could hear the fans in the stands saying, "You niggers better leave before it turns dark!"

Little did they know, once they started trouble the guys on our team had something for them! It was going to be an all out war once the fans and the other team started trouble.

Blacks were tired of dealing with the KKK from Smithfield, N.C. When you drove through the town you would always get stopped and given a ticket and you better not say a bad word to the officer or you were going down to the station and get your ass whipped.

I don't know how the atmosphere is in Smithfield today, but I do know that when I drive through there, I'm very careful not to break any rules...the Klan still exists. In 1992, the Klan's marched through downtown Kinston heading to Grifton, North Carolina.

I was surprised but in the first amendment, it is a clause that says, 'You have the freedom to assemble,' but the policemen were nervous about the situation. I even seen the Kinston S.W.A.T Team on top of buildings because they felt there was going to be a fight but to my surprise it went alright.

I really didn't start to learn about racism until I started school; I guess my grandmother never took time out to tell us about racism, maybe because she didn't want to pollute our minds. The older folks knew about it but I guess the younger children didn't know about it. We were to busy playing in the neighborhood. The only thing I knew was blacks stayed in one section of the town and whites stayed in another section of the town.

When I was going to Lewis Elementary School, my music teacher was a white lady named, Mrs. Edwards. She slapped me in the face with her hands for talking - she will always regret doing that.

My mother was staying in D.C. at the time and I think she had just come home to visit for a couple of days. I think my Uncle Jay was either a guidance counselor or he taught the sixth grade. I came home and told my mother what had happened. The next day she went to school with me and was ready to jump on the teacher. I think the principal of the school had to call Jay from his office to cool things off. Of course Jay knew how his sister was - wild and crazy. The only thing I know is that Mrs. Edwards never put her hands on me again.

I wasn't the only student Mrs. Edwards slapped. She slapped another student in the face and his nose started to bleed. The student's name was Trenton; he was a year older than I was. How this lady got away with this shit I don't know. Trent's aunt was a teacher at the school.

As I've grown older I can look back and see there was racism at the swimming pool. The blacks would go swim at Holloway or Lovett Hines Pool and the whites would go swim at Emma Webb Pool. If blacks went to Emma Webb Pool, the staff didn't make you get out of the pool but somehow, you knew you didn't belong there.

When I got older my family ended up leaving the projects and moving right around the corner from Emma Webb Pool. There were several movie theaters we attended. Most of the blacks attended the State Theater on South Queen Street; I would pay fifty cents to get in the movie. I never saw a white person at that theater, I only seen whites at the Paramount and the Park Theater. Both places charged seventy-five cents to get in the movie. When we didn't have the money we would sneak in the movies. I can even recall me and my friend Antray trying to sneak in the movies.

There was an alley located in the back of the Paramount Theater; it was easy to open the back door of the theater. One Sunday when we didn't have any money, we went in the back of the Paramount Theater and opened the door while the movie was playing; we crawled on our knees through the curtains until we found us a seat and mixed in with the crowd. What we didn't know was that in the balcony, one of the staff members seen us come through the door.

While we were in our seats, two staff members came, a man named Grip and a lady named Susie. Grip pointed us out and Antray took off running; before I could take off running the staff grabbed me.

"Susie, call the police!!!!!!!!!!!!!!!!!!!!!!!!!" Grip said when we got up to the front office.

My heart started beating real fast because I knew what was going to happen when I got home.

"You must have got me mixed up with someone else," I told Grip.

"No I didn't! I saw you and your friend sneaking in through the back door!"

I looked down below my feet and seen a lot of ticket stubs on the floor, I bent down as if I were tying my shoe and slipped one of the ticket stubs in my pocket.

When the police came, Grip told the police I had broken in through the back door of the movie with one of my friends but the other friend ran off.

"I didn't know the man that ran. I didn't sneak into the movies. I have my ticket stub here in my pocket." I said to the police.

Susie looked at my ticket stub and compared it with the tickets they had sold that day and said, "He can't be the one because his ticket stub matches with what we sold today."

All of a sudden I got brave…"I told you all that you had the wrong person."

Susie said, "Grip, let him go back into the movies."

The police left and I went back inside the movies. My heart was beating so hard that I couldn't enjoy the movie thinking that they might come out and get me again; the name of the movie that was playing was called, *'The Greatest'* featuring Muhammad Ali. I felt like I had just gotten out of the *greatest* trouble that I had ever been in.

CHAPTER 13

I Was a Devious Kid

When I was growing up in Carver Courts, I did some devious things that I consider devious. My friends and I used to go around and ring peoples door bells - before they would open the door we would take off running. Doing these types of devious things was funny. It was so funny that we added more fun to it. We would sit bottles at people's doors and ring the door bell and take off running and when they opened the door the bottles would break. We would be somewhere in the bushes laughing our asses off. If my grandmother ever found out that I'd done these things growing up, she would be mad because she taught me how to behave myself.

My friends and I stole little petty things from the stores. Things like moon pies, oatmeal cakes, and potato chips. I remember going to Mr. Keebler's store - we knew he couldn't half see; we'd steal things right in front of his face. None of the kids needed to steal anything because we all came from good back grounds. Our family supplied us with what we needed. It's ironic that the people who don't need anything are the main people that go out and get into trouble for the hell of it. This is not cool!

I'm ashamed of my past and if you are reading this book and you have done the same things that I've done, you should be ashamed too!

My stealing days ended quickly at least I thought. I think kids do things because of peer pressure and the challenge of, 'let me do this to see whether or not I can get away with it.' The last time I ever stole anything was at a store called 'Rayners.'

We all always heard that Mr. Rayners was a Klansman but whether or not that was true is another story; I'm not going to try to validate something I don't know. Me and one of my friends name Wheezy went to Rayners Supermarket to steal things for the party we used to have with the kids in the neighborhood. Wheezy was the ring leader, we would pitch in ten or fifteen cents to purchase cookies, hotdogs, hotdog rolls, chilly, ketchup, mustard, and chips. Me and Wheezy would steal most of the items and go to the counter and pay for the rest of the items. That was a bold move on our part, we were paying for the items, while we had stolen items in the waist of our pants.

On this one occasion we went into Mr. Rayners store; I think I'd stolen a can of meat or something. I can't remember what it was but I remember Wheezy and I were right beside each other; Wheezy was smooth when he was stealing. He would steal, and both of us would cover by looking to see if anyone was looking.

He said, "Hey man there goes Mr. Rayners, go 'head on and get that out of your pants and put it back!"

Wheezy put his things back real smooth and walked away; I was trying to put mine back but somehow the can food got stuck between my belt; I was trying so, so hard to get those can foods out of my belt and Rayners caught me…

"I ought to call the police," he said, "Bert, call the police!"

Bert said, "Naw I'm not going to call the police, I know his mother and I'll pay for it myself. Then I'll tell his mother on him."

Bert knew that my mother didn't stay in North Carolina anymore but she knew I stayed with my grandmother. Bert was a small nice white lady that really helped people out. She got along with blacks. Her husband was a police officer and she and my mother were very close.

Mrs. Bert called the house but my grandmother wasn't there so my Uncle Hamm came and picked me up and took me home. When my grandmother found out what I had done, she beat the hell out of me and my stealing days were over with. Until this day I have never stolen anything again.

I remember when my brother Pete and my cousin Eric got caught stealing. This incident took place on a Saturday. I came in the house with my basketball and my grandmother was ironing clothes in the pantry; my Aunt Denderant was in the kitchen.

Denderant said, "What were you doing out stealing?"

I didn't have a clue what she was talking about.

"How did you get away from the police station so fast? Jay just left to go down to the police station to pick you up…I don't know why the police let you go when we told them we were sending someone down there to pick you up."

Denderant hit me side the head.

"I wasn't stealing I just came off the basketball court!"

"You are lying!"

I couldn't convince her that I wasn't stealing. My grandmother rolled her eyes and said, "Garry what did you steal?"

"No ma'am, I didn't steal anything."

After my grandmother asked me the question about stealing, Jay had walked in the house with Pete. Pete was the one that was stealing. Denderant, nor my grandmother could believe it. Pete was a laid back, "A and B" student that never got into trouble and never caused any headaches for my family. When the police called the house and said we have your grandson down at the station for stealing and could you please come and pick him up, immediately my family thought it was me. They appeared as though they were disappointed that it was Pete and not me.

Jay feelings were hurt because Pete had asked Jay 'if he would give him some money to go down town to buy him something.' Pete had the money but he didn't pay for the items. He and my cousin Eric was on a roll.

Eric managed not to get caught but Pete told them that Eric was stealing too. My grandmother called her nephew Johnny Lee; this was Eric's father and told him that Eric was down town stealing with Pete.

Earlier in the book, I said my grandmother would step in and stop my aunts and uncle from disciplining us if it was petty but she didn't stop Jay this time.

Jay took Pete upstairs and started beating the hell out of him with his belt. Jay was beating Pete so hard *I* started crying. I left the house and walked a few steps away. I heard Johnny Lee beating the hell out of Eric and Eric was screaming just as loud as Pete. We stayed in the 8th building and Eric and his parents stayed in the 9th building. I walked in the cemetery that was across the street from Carver Courts and started thinking about what had gone on between Eric and Pete. I was very surprised about Pete stealing. Neither Pete nor Eric was able to go out the house for about a week.

If parents were to start back disciplining their kids the way *we* were disciplined, a lot of kids would not be in as much trouble as they are in today.

Today parents are afraid of their kids, they are afraid of what social service would do to them. The only thing the kids have to say when their kids are being discipline is, 'they are going to call social service' and the discipline stops. We have allowed the government to frighten us when it comes to disciplining our children. Yet, the government wants to know why these black kids are the way they are (out of control).

I understand that some parents *go over board* when they are disciplining their kids and social services have to step in. I'm not making light of kids being abused, but some of the things are not child abuse. If that was the case all of our parents in the past should be locked up because they whipped some ass back in the day.

I notice that most of the kids that weren't disciplined when they got into trouble are either dead, in prison, or on drugs. The shame of it all is that we have become soooooo society wise. Meaning that we allow the government to step in, when in the old days if a child got his behind beat, he would never think about calling the police.

We didn't think of calling the police and was afraid of the repercussions that would occur if we dialed the police number; you had to move or go stay with the policeman that came to the house that you called. It is not the same today. The school teacher is afraid to spank the children; when we were spanked at school, someone told our parents and you got a whipping from your parents that same day.

CHAPTER 14

Legal Hustler

Growing up as a kid, I was what you would call a *'legal hustler'*. I made money any way I could but it was always legal...it all started in Elementary School. The schools would have the 'Candy Selling Drives' for different charities or towards something the school needed. If the students wanted to participate, they could volunteer to take a case of candy bars home and sell them.

At the end of the candy drive, the students could win prizes for selling the most candy or cookies or whatever the school was selling. You had 1st place, 2nd place, and 3rd place; of course, I wanted 1st place.

I would take a case of candy home and go door to door asking people until they wanted to buy some candy. The candy bar was small but the school would charge a dollar for each candy bar. Most of the people that bought the candy, knew they could go to the store and buy four candy bars for what we were charging, but it was for a good cause which is why the people bought them.

I didn't let the 'hard customers' get away easy. I had my own game and charm for them. I would just smile and say, "I want to win a prize sir or madam, could you just buy the candy so I can win."

Sometimes after I got through talking, the customer would buy *three* bars instead of one bar - they couldn't resist what I found out later on, was called, 'charm'. My grandmother Tessie Jones didn't get off easy either. She would take about ten bars to work and sell them; within a day or two, a case of candy was sold. I would go back to school and ask for two more cases and then it turned into three cases...I was on a roll. The teachers wouldn't say who was in the lead but I knew I had to be in the top three because I wasn't going to let anyone win over me in getting that 1st place prize.

After the contest was over, the school would hold some kind of awards day and announce who sold the most candy and when they said 'Garry Jones', I walked my cool ass up there on stage and accepted that cheap prize that they had in store for me. I can't remember what the prize was but I know it was cheap. I had sold about $100 worth of candy and probably only got a $5 prize.

I would go home and tell my grandmother that I had won; she was more excited than I was. My grandmother knew I was a special kid but she didn't know how special I was. I not only sold candy in the hood, but me and my buddy Vince a.k.a. Bunny would borrow his father's lawn mower and go cut grass and make plenty of money.

I would knock on the door and ask, "Do you want me to cut your grass for you?"

"Yes," some would say.

I turned to Bunny and said, "Let's do it!"

My job was to police the yards and pick up any rocks, big branches, cans and anything that would mess up the blade of the lawn mower. When I was finished, Bunny would cut the person's yard as if it was someone getting a haircut at a barber shop. That's how good Bunny could cut a yard.

Bunny's father would ask for a cut of the money because we were using his lawn mower, but we fixed that real quick; we gave him his cut but we kept cutting every week or every two weeks and saved the money. Eventually we had enough money saved up to buy us a new lawn mower and his father couldn't get any of our money.

When Bunny and I weren't cutting grass we would pop popcorn and make lemonade and take it out on the basketball court, then we'd sell it to the guys who were playing ball, even though both of us were athletes as well. We made our money first then we played ball afterwards.

The other guys in the hood would have their hustle but they couldn't take our customers…*their* customers were loyal to us. I had my own hustle on the side *without* Bunny.

People in the hood as well as most other people, drank those Pepsi and Dr. Peppers, especially the older folks, they would put peanuts in their sodas. I would have me a grocery cart and go to every door and ask for people bottles. I would then sell the bottles to a man named, Mr. Moe. He would give me three cents for every bottle and then he would take the bottles to the plant and they would give him five cents for every bottle.

When I wasn't selling bottles, I would be selling Kings Chapel Tea, that's the church that my grandmother was a member of. They had their own tea bags in their boxes with their church name on them. It was only right that I sold the tea because my grandmother hustled for me and so I hustled to help her out. Nickel and dimming wasn't good enough for me so I had to step my hustle game up...

My Aunt Colleen (Mavis) would read the Jet magazines and cut out things that the magazines were advertising for you to sale. This particular advertisement that was popular was getting people social security number and asking them do they want their social security cards made out of medal with the government symbol on them. I would take the orders for $2 and my aunt would mail the company $1 for each order taken and I kept a dollar.

I became rich doing that because hell, you had to sell a lot of bottles to make a dollar and I made a dollar with one order.

Of course my aunt wouldn't let me spend all of my money at one time so she would take some of the money and save it for me. I remember my cousin Annie Mae was in high school and they had the Miss Cotillion Contest, black folks call it Miss Cotillion Ball, but white folks call it The Debutante Ball; guess who they called on to help Ann to compete and win third place...they called *'The Hustler'*.

My grandmother was the best cook in the world and even though I don't like Sweet Potato Pies, my grandmother would make the pies and I (*'The Hustler'*) would go out and sell them like hotcakes. Ann probably would have gotten 1st place if my grandmother would have made her Banana Pudding and told me to go out and sell them.

The 1st, 2nd and 3rd place wasn't that much different. I wished she would have gotten 1st place because I worked my butt off. Third place was not good enough for me, but the fact is, if more money was donated and if we didn't have to sell pies, Ann could have taken the grand prize home.

CHAPTER 15

Falling Out in the Cucumber Field

Growing up in the projects, Mr. Aaron, one of my friend's father, would have his own truck and would recruit guys from the neighborhood who wanted to work in the tobacco field and cucumber fields in the country.

I had always wanted to go but I had asthma and asking my grandmother could I go was down right crazy…I knew the answer.

The fellows who went got paid on Friday's…they would work from sunup to sundown and on Friday's they would flash the money they made. Of course my little $5 a week couldn't compare to the $100 they made.

Aaron's son Vince a.k.a. Bunny would always take me downtown with him when he spent his money. He would buy his school clothes and treat me to hot dogs and sodas at a store called, 'Roses.' Bunny would also give me five dollars to spend which made me have ten dollars.

My mind couldn't stand seeing them with all of that money and I couldn't get in on some of the action.

One morning around 6:00 a.m., I decided to get up and sneak out of the window to catch the cucumber truck; of course the people who work in the cucumber field didn't make as much as the people who worked in the tobacco field.

Little did I know that you couldn't work all day in one hundred degree weather and not have eaten breakfast and have plenty to drink.

When I got to the cucumber field, eating cucumbers was my breakfast until I began to get sick and real dizzy. Gail and Aaron's daughter went to the white man to let them know what was happening to me. The white man called the ambulance and told me not to come back.

On the way to the hospital, I think Ann and Gail rode in the ambulance with me to the hospital. While riding in the ambulance, I could feel myself getting better because of the air conditioning.

When I got to the hospital, someone had to call my grandmother; I don't know who called but my mind was racing with the thought of what she was going to do or say.

When you go to the hospital, they don't let you go right away. You have to stay there while they run tests before you are released...I think Jay came to pick me up.

When I got home, my grandmother looked at me and rolled her eyes and told me, "Sit at the kitchen table and eat your supper (dinner)."

She had cooked fried chicken and some pork n' beans; that was the best chicken and pork n' beans I had in my life.

CHAPTER 16

Carver Courts Socials

Carver Courts Center is where the socials were held at. The center was a recreational center where kids could come in and play ping pong, cards, and shoot pool and on the weekends at night is when the 'socials' were held.

Carver Courts socials were the bomb and everybody from across town used to come over to our social. When I was a kid I was told not to go to the socials, because I was too young and a fight may break out. In all actuality, it was very rare that you would find a fight at the social. Everyone was trying to *out dance* one another.

I remember when the staff at the Carver Courts Center first painted the 'Soul Train' line, the Soul Train line was red, black and green; the soul train picture looked like the same picture that was on the show 'Soul Train' from back in the 70's.

The socials were held mostly on Friday and Saturday nights. You had to pay a quarter to get in but I would sneak in and if I didn't sneak in, there was someone at the door who knew me and knew I was too young to be in there because you had to be sixteen to get in, but they didn't say anything.

The staff member in charge of opening up the center was Josh Wooten. Josh would give instructions not to let anyone in if they weren't sixteen and then Josh would leave and come back in time to lock up the place.

When it was time to go down and dance on the soul train line, it was just like on TV. The girls would line up on one side and the guys would line up on the other side and each would go down the soul train line jamming, of course I was young and couldn't dance, as a matter of fact I can't dance now, but I went down the line anyway with my moves.

The socials would end at like twelve midnight. They ran, mostly everybody out and then the staff would clean up and the crowd would go hang on the block and that's when your fights broke out. A lot of people used to look after me especially King George; he made sure no one touched me until I got home.

I remember when King George and Jerry Alston had shootouts. King George was representing Carver Courts (The Block) and Jerry Alston was representing Mitchell Wooten Courts (The Front). Theses two guys didn't like each other and when they seen each other they would take their guns out and stand behinds cars and shoot at each other. Needless to say, neither one of them got shot. It reminded you of the 'Wild, Wild West,' they had their fights as well.

I really don't think they were trying to hit each other when they were shooting, they were sending a message that you stay over on your side of town and I will stay over on my side of town.

The *legends* in Carver Courts were people like King George, my Uncle Jay, my Uncle Hamm, Hook Jones, Johnny Tuff, James Freeman, Nellie Q, Zeek Raspberry, Pop Hussey, Shack Hart, Kemoe Dixon, Tyrone Warren, Don Pitman, Dooley

Wilkes, James Bay-boy Irvin, Scull, Wink Eye. Jim Danny, Lee Lee and a lot of other brothers.

King George was the best in getting you what you needed, King George would take your order of anything you wanted and come back the same day with what you ordered. King George is the only person that stole shit and never got caught.

Someone wanted a T.V. and King George went to some appliance place and while he was in there he went to the front counter and asked someone, "Can you open the door so I can take my T.V. out?"

The workers didn't know that they were opening the door for King George to steal their merchandise. King George was the Robin Hood of Carver Courts. He and his boys, Thomas, Ken, and Larry Godwin would break in a grocery store and steal all the groceries and come back to Carver Courts and fire up the grill and feed anyone who wanted to eat for free. We were eating steaks, pork chops, chicken, whatever you named, King George and his crew had it, they were drinking wine, beer, sodas, and smoking cigarettes. King George never got caught in action, but he always went to prison because someone snitched on him but he refused to snitch on anyone else. If anyone came over to Carver Courts and didn't stay there and if they started trouble, King George would take out his sawed off shotgun and go looking for the people. He also fought with his hands.

The legends also used to fight *each other*: King George and James Freeman, James Freeman and Johnny Cool, Johnny Cool and Lawrence Gooding and the list go on.

CHAPTER 17

There Was Something Different About Me

I was a different kid, not because I suffered from depression, asthma, and ulcers and not because I was made to go to Church, Vacation Bible School and Sunday School, but I wasn't satisfied when I didn't get the answers to the questions I asked of people.

My school teachers would always say, "You ask too many questions." There were other adults that weren't teachers that would say, "Man you ask too many damn questions."

Little did I know that I also had another side to me and that side was spiritual? I can't say that side came from church even though I had to go, but I would cut up in church and couldn't tell you what the sermons were about. When I was small or a kid, I would often find me a spot somewhere by myself and sing to God...I don't mean singing words to God because I couldn't sing, but I would sing God a hymn.

To this day, I never forgot how the tune went. I have always known that God would be a part of my life but I never knew in what way. He didn't keep me on this earth for nothing. I don't know why God is allowing me to still live in this world because if it was up to me, I would have clocked out a long time ago but committing suicide is not the way to get to heaven.

I often pray and ask God what is my purpose in this world. I'm still praying to God for the answer to that question but I still don't have an answer. Maybe if I stop breaking those 'Ten Commandments' and align myself with his will, maybe I would hear from him.

There is an old saying, *dying is easy but living is hard*, especially when you are trying to do the right thing. Every time that I thought I would get myself together something in this world would always get my attention. I found out later on in life that is how satan works. When you try to live God's way, satan will fight hard to take you away from him. You notice I spelled satan without a capital's; I refuse to give satan any credit. His name doesn't deserve to be spelled correctly.

When I was a child I would always go to the cemetery and talk to God but he never answered me back. Some people say they can hear God's voice, they say his voice sounds like water coming out of an ocean. I got to be able to hear this before I can believe it. I have heard that God speaks through the Holy Spirit when he wants to talk with you, but whatever the case maybe He still hasn't told me what I'm here for. Until he tells me, I guess I will still be listening out for him. I should have been dead a long time ago and later on in this book, you will see what I'm talking about.

CHAPTER 18

Leaving Carver Courts

Front Row, Left to Right, of Course Me With My Cool 9 Year Old Ass,
Cousin Sharon, Brother Pete, and Sister Lisa
Second Row Uncle Steve Mason

Moving out of Carver Courts was one of the hardest things to deal with in my life; the thought of leaving my friends was terrifying.

It was January 14, 1977, on a Saturday evening when we actually moved. I lived in Carver Courts twelve years, eleven months and two weeks. I was mad as hell. I didn't want to live in a house! I wanted to live in the projects!

This was a devastating blow for me I didn't know how to handle not waking up going on the basketball court and playing in the Carver Courts Center. My family tried to make up for it by putting a basketball court in our back yard.

The only thing good about waking up January 15, 1977, was the Super Bowl that was on. The Oakland Raiders and the Minnesota Vikings were playing. The Cowboys weren't playing – they were and *still is* my team. The Cowboys had just lost the year before to the Pittsburg Steelers when Jackie Smith dropped that touchdown pass in the end zone.

I wanted to be back in Carver Courts so bad that I literally road my bike in the morning back to Carver Courts to walk to school with my friends. I didn't give damn about catching the bus to school. After school I walked back to Carver Courts as if I still lived there. I played with my friends and rode my bike back to my new home.

Denderant, my grandmother and the rest of the family were elated, their dreams were to leave the projects but my dreams were to stay in the projects until death. I was still a kid, I didn't know any better. What my family was doing was trying to own something instead of paying rent all the time. I always said once I got older I would go back and live in Carver Courts but that never happened.

A kid couldn't understand this concept until they got older. The longer we stayed in the new house, the more I was able to adjust to my new environment. It took me about three years to adjust. Whenever the New Year would come around, I would try my best to bring in the New Year's at Carver Courts. It was hard to forget where I came from. When the clock struck 12, I would holler, "Happy New Years!!!!!!!!!!!!!!!!!!!!" Then I would walk back to my house which was fifteen minutes away.

I didn't realize how blessed I was, the brick home was nice and beautiful and we had our own fire place, I was too blind to see what God bless our family to get, because I was blinded by Carver Courts.

Me and Pete still had to share bedrooms. My grandmother had the master bedroom, Denderant had the room bigger than the master bedroom and me and Pete had the smaller room; Ann, had gone to college and Mavis had moved to Raleigh, North Carolina. Jay had already moved out but he was still the man of the house because we still got punished whenever we got in trouble or our grades dropped.

I really didn't appreciate what I had because I didn't like real food unless it was fried chicken, pork chops, and mashed potatoes. I loved junk food and that is why I stayed sick all the time. The doctor used to tell my grandmother that I needed to take vitamins.

On Friday evenings, I knew what the menu was, fish that still had the eyeball in it, cornbread, and maybe cabbage. My grandmother used to give me money every Friday because she knew I wasn't going to eat what she cooked. I took those couples of dollars and went to McDonalds.

I must admit my grandmother spoiled me.

It was hard for my grandmother to stop cooking those big meals after we moved into our house. I guess when you've been cooking for a long period of time for a big family; you still continue to prepare big meals. My grandmother was happy to move. I could see it all over her body; she had that swagger when she got around her friends and was proud to go to work. She would wake me up and give me lunch money and a couple more pennies to get me a cinnamon roll or a milkshake for lunch.

She made sure her grandchildren *had* even if she had to go without and when I went on my sporting trips or just school trips in general, she would make sure that I had money. She would soon get her money back during the summer when I got a job.

CHAPTER 19

The Trainer

In the fall of 1977 I was a trainer for Kinston High Football Team. I was under the supervision of a teacher named Mr. Johnny Shepherd. Mr. Shepherd gave me, Tony Hill and Eric Koonce the trainer's job.

He taught us how to wrap ankles and attend to minor injuries for the varsity football team. Mr. Shepherd made us feel like we could do anything. Everyone didn't make the traveling squad, even some of the players, but Mr. Shepherd carried his trainers every where he went. I was his main man. The only thing I hated about my position was giving water to the team during game night.

Whenever it was a timeout on the football field, somehow Eric would dodge this job, he would be somewhere else. Eric has always been slick ever since we were kids; he and I were second cousins. The players would ask you to bring the water out on the field, and when you would run with the water, they would tell you to go back and before you could go back to the sidelines, they would tell you to bring the water back again. I used to get mad as hell because at that time they had a big five gallon container of water with about five nozzles on them and the pump in the middle.

In order for the water to come out of the nozzles, you had to keep pumping the pump until the water came up to the nozzles. I used to have to run with that container until the water came out during timeout. When the players were *winning*, I would bring the water on the field and they used to be happy and start joking during timeouts, but when they were *losing*, they would tell you, "Get that damn water out of here!"

I used to be pissed at those players, so after the season I said I wasn't going to be a trainer anymore. It was good while it lasted but I wasn't going to take that abuse.

After the season, I went to work for my father, first I started working only on Saturday cleaning up the garage for two hours getting paid $75 dollars a month. Considering I wasn't a trainer anymore my father asked me to work after school from 4 p.m. to 6 p.m. and I did.

When I would get out of school I would go back to Carver Courts where my cousin lived and change clothes and then I would walk across the cemetery to the shop. My responsibilities were to clean the bathroom, sweep the floor, and clean the tools. It was still quiet between my father and me because we didn't have that much to say. He might quiz me on some math to see what I knew. I would answer his questions and continue to clean up.

I tried out for my eighth grade basketball team and Coach Little cut me during the final cut. I was crushed. I actually went home and cried my heart out. My father asked me did I want to work full time instead of just Saturdays. I really didn't, but I loved money and said, 'Yes.'

I would leave school (weekdays) and go to work. To tell you the truth all of my work was done in the first forty-five minutes and I really didn't have anything to do until 5:45 p.m. When the shop was beginning to close, then that's when all the sweeping was done. My father and I still didn't have much of a conversation. I would look at him as he strolled around being cool with that cigarette in his mouth.

There was a song that came on the radio called, *Everyone Plays the Fool.* I forgot the group that sung the song, but when my father would hear that song, he would get his 'pimp walk' on. My grandfather would just stare at me all the time, he never would say anything. When customers would come to the shop and see me, they would say "Meat, that's got to be your g-damn son, he look just like you, Meat you can't deny him!!!! That little m-f looks just like you."

"Young man, what's your mother name?" This is what they would ask.

I remember walking down Queen Street and a man looked at me and said, "Son, I don't know who you are but, you got to be Meat Dove's son."

"Yes, I am," is all I would say.

My father had a temper back then but he was also a hustler, no my father wasn't a hustler in the sense that causes you to go to jail, but he knew how to *make money*.

I remember him saying "Goldwater, go over to that house across from the cemetery and clean it up."

He gave me the key and I didn't ask any questions. When I got over there, I would see beer bottles, cigarettes, and playing cards. I cleaned it up and still didn't ask any questions and every week I would go over and clean up, often when I cleaned up I would find change lying on the floor. One day it hit me, this is a gambling house, but of course I never told my father I knew what the house was, it was obvious.

On this one particular day my father found out that the school was having teachers work day (which meant I didn't have to go to school). The next day, he called me and said, "I want you to come to work at 8 a.m. to 6 p.m."

I didn't like this shit because whenever we didn't have to go to school, I wanted to stay and hang out with my friends. I told him I would be in. When I reported to work; I didn't have a smile on my face.

"What's wrong with you?"

"Nothing," I said; went and got the broom and swept a little bit.

Right before he took his lunch break, my father said, "Goldwater (Nickname), I want you to go upstairs and get the swing blade and cut down the weeds over where the old junk cars were."

When he came back from lunch, I could smell alcohol on his breath.

"Goldwater, I thought I told you to get that damn swing blade and cut those damn weeds down."

Mr. Dove (my grandfather) didn't pay me to do that, he only paid me to clean the tools, sweep the floor, and clean the bathroom."

"What did you say!"

I repeated it back to him.

"If you don't take your m-f ass up stairs and get that g-d swing blade and cut down those weeds, I will beat your m-f ass!"

I dropped the rag that I had in my hands and walked away.

"Bring your g-d ass back here!"

I kept walking and then I could hear his footsteps, so I took off running and when I turned around, I seen him take his cap off of his head and he started chasing me through the cemetery but he couldn't catch me. As a matter of fact one time, he was gaining ground on me because I was scared and my legs felt numb but he still wasn't able to catch me, I knew he was going straight to my cousin's apartment in Carver Courts because he knew I changed clothes over there but I out-smarted him and ran into Mrs. Sue's apartment.

My father ran to my cousin's house like I expected him to do, when he got there, my cousin told him, "You need to leave before I call my father, because Goldwater isn't here." I told Mrs. Sue to call my house and tell my grandmother that my father was trying to jump on me. My grandmother sent my Uncle Hamm to come pick me up.

I was petrified even though I knew I was safe over Mrs. Sue's house, but somehow I thought my father would find me before Hamm got there to pick me up. If my father would have found me, he probably would have beaten the hell out of me with his hands. He was just that mad.

When Hamm came I felt safe, he took me back home and my grandmother asked me what happened. I explained to my grandmother that my father was hollering and cursing at me, of course my grandmother didn't say anything, but to my surprise my Aunt Denderant, who didn't like my father said, "Who do you supposed to be, you are not too good to be hollered at."

My grandmother said, "He doesn't have any business hollering at that boy and he doesn't have to work over at the shop."

I knew my grandmother had my back.

"Go to your room and finish out your lessons (homework)," she said.

A couple hours later, I heard the doorbell ring and when my grandmother went to the door I heard my father say, "Hello Mrs. Jones."

I didn't hear my grandmother say anything.

My father said, "Is Goldwater home?"

"Yes, he is here."

"May I speak to him Ma'am?"

"If he wants to talk with you he can but if not, you can't see him…Garry, your father is here, do you want to talk to him?"

"Yes, I will talk to him."

My father and I went outside by the tree and talked. I could still smell the alcohol on his breath. The first thing that came out of his mouth was, 'g-damn boy, you can run.'

He said, "I'm sorry about what happen today, I want you to come back to work."

"I don't want to and besides I'm going out for the football team in a couple of weeks."

"You don't need to play any football. You need to work, are you coming back to work or what?"

I told him no and went back in the house. I could tell my father was mad. He took this personally; we didn't speak to each other for about a whole year. He would see me on the streets and wouldn't say anything or speak and neither would I.

I can remember going on Queen Street to shoot pool; my father walked in and never opened his mouth to say anything, my cousin Eric would say, "Boy, there is your father, go say something to him." But, I didn't I just kept on playing pool and didn't do a good job at that because Eric was kicking my behind and taking my money. After my father walked in the pool hall, I lost all concentration. It does feel weird to see your father and he doesn't speak to you.

Of course my Uncle Hamm would be in the pool hall noticing everything that was taking place; he did notice that we weren't speaking. One of my friends name Vick who hung with my father, would say, 'What's up, Gold.' I would shake my head as to say, 'Nothing much.' It's ironic that even though my father and I weren't speaking he would always show up for one of my sporting events.

When I was running Junior Olympics I came to the bleachers to change my track shoes and seen my father, we both looked at each other but we didn't speak. I spoke to Victor Olds, a classmate of mine and a friend to my father but not a word was uttered to my father.

CHAPTER 20

My First Real Job

My first real job was probably in 1978 while I was still in eighth grade. The city had a summer program called, Green Lamp. This program helped the youth of families with low income that was fourteen years old and older, get a summer job; this gave the children something to do and this was also another tool with keeping young children out of trouble. An idle mind is the devils' workshop, meaning if you don't have anything to do, then satan will put thoughts in your mind and convince you to go get in trouble.

Most of the summer programs are cut out now; take notice of how more and more young children are getting into trouble; *how can you expect young children not to get in trouble when they don't have anything to do.*

Out of all of the government programs, why cut the summer job program for the youth. It appears that the government wants our children to get in trouble.

Mayor Marion Berry was known for ensuring the summer program for hiring young children was not cut out. Once he went to prison the new mayor came in and cut the summer programs for the youth. What a dumb move, and it was a black mayor at that, she knows the plight of the black youth but then again she may have not been part of the black struggle. It's hard for anyone to understand the plight of the black youth when you have never been in their environment; this includes our own black people.

I'm not using this as an excuse because parents burden the responsibilities as well. You have to know where your kids are located at all times. It's hard to do this with one parent but this mission can be accomplished.

Getting back to my first job, when I was hired in the Green Lamp program, they assigned me to work at Caswell

Center. This was a center for severely mentally challenged people.

It was my understanding that the land Caswell Center was built on was supposed to have been for a university. As a matter of fact this place supposed to have been the home for East Carolina University. This should give you insight on how big Caswell Center is. I have been around mentally challenged people before but not to this agree. We had a couple of mentally challenged people in Carver Courts that I became used to.

One of the guys stayed in the back of me, his name was Fountain; Fountain was an older guy around thirty-five to forty years old with a mind of an eight year old. Fountain used to wear his dungarees outfit and you would never see him without a Pepsi and a bag of peanuts, as a matter of fact Fountain used to put peanuts in his Pepsi soda.

It was easy to get Fountain wound up, the only thing you had to tell Fountain is that someone was talking about his mother, Mrs. Hayes. Whenever the fellows didn't like someone in the neighborhood or wanted Fountain to jump on them, we would tell Fountain, "Hey man, Gino was talking about your mother."

Fountain would grab Gino by the collars and say, "I heard you were talking about my mother *last year*."

Gino scared ass would tell Fountain, "That was last year, why are you jumping on me this year."

Fountain weighed around eighty pounds, but he was strong as an ox. Everyone was scared of Fountain. When he came to me with that bullshit about me talking about his mother, I would tell him, "You jump on me if you want to, I'm going to tell my Uncle Hamm to whip your ass and go tell Mrs. Hayes."

Little did Fountain know that I was afraid of him, but I couldn't let him know; I befriended Fountain just in case someone wanted to jump on me. First I would buy him a Pepsi and some peanuts and then he would settle down. Everyday Fountain looked for his Pepsi and Peanuts and sometimes Fountain would grab your pant pockets to see if you had any money.

"Damn, man I don't have money *everyday*."

He wasn't trying to hear that, but he wouldn't try to jump on me if I didn't have any money.

I recall this very special day about him and my best friend Antray. Someone told Fountain that Antray was talking about his mother.

"Look, Fountain I wasn't talking about your mother; this isn't true."

Fountain wasn't going for it. Antray hauled off and knocked the hell out of Fountain and it was on and popping then.

After Antray hit Fountain, he took off running; Fountain was behind him gaining ground. As I mentioned earlier Fountain was about thirty-five to forty years old with a mind of an eight year old and Fountain could outrun the average deer. He was chasing Antray and the fellows thought he was going to catch Antray but Antray was getting closer to home and the closer he got to home Fountain was gaining on him, he was one yard behind him. Antray mother was at the door and seen

Antray running towards the house to get away from Fountain. Antray's mother Mrs. Christine (Rest in Peace) held the door for him to come through and when he got two yards from the house Antray dived in the house like a swimmer and Mrs. Christine shut the door because Fountain dived in after him but Fountain hit the door so hard that it knocked his old ass out. The fellows were laughing their asses off.

Until this day, I believe after Antray hit Fountain, he didn't run from him anymore. I think Fountain was surprised that someone stood up to him. It is my understanding that Fountain was at Caswell Center at one time but his mother decided she didn't want him out there and she raised Fountain at home; Mrs. Hayes was determined not to give her child away because he was mentally challenged.

There was another mentally challenged brother in the neighborhood named Linwood. Linwood had some form of education, he used to ride the *little yellow bus*, this was a great thing that his family did; they cared enough about Linwood to get him some type of education. I think Fountain was a little more challenged than Linwood was. Every mentally challenged person can not fit in the same category.

Linwood was a hustler like I was, he would sell bottles, rake yards and do what he could to make money. Linwood also could count. As a matter of fact, today Linwood is still doing the same chores that he was doing in Carver Courts. Fountain is still being cared for by his sister in Baltimore.

The last time I seen Fountain was at a family function, he can't see that well but he is still wearing his dungarees and drinking Pepsi. I walked up to Fountain and asked did he know who I was and he said, "Yes."

Fountain grabbed my stomach and shouted to everyone in the room, "Goldwater has a big stomach!!!!!!! Goldwater has a big stomach!!!!!!!!"

Getting back to working at Caswell Center, I was hired around June 1978 and went for orientation the next week. I can remember my grandmother dropping me off to my first orientation.

When she turned down Pecan Lane I got excited because I knew I would be bringing home a nice paycheck and I knew I would be able to help my grandmother. I got paid every two weeks and I would give her half of my check. I didn't mind giving it to her considering how much she did for me.

The Caswell Center is located on Pecan Lane in Kinston, N.C. After the orientation the supervisor that interviewed me told me I would be assigned to the Kendal three or Kendal one building.

When I reported to work it was on and popping, the mentally challenged residents gave me a run for my money! These residents were just like Fountain but they were challenged more than Fountain and they were a lot *stronger*!

My first day, I was assigned to gather the residents together for lunch, this was a task because some came to the table and some was out doing God knows what. My shift was 11 a.m. to 7:30 p.m. We had to be very careful dealing with the residents. Some were able to feed themselves and others were not. During my shift I was the only male working amongst a couple of females. Theses females didn't have the strength to handle these residents and who did they call on when some of the residents would go to fighting...me that's who - a 120 pound guy.

I was pretty strong myself but the residents were *three times* stronger than I was. Some of them would get out of their chair and *cold cock* the shit out of another resident; the resident that was hit acted as though he didn't feel a thing.

After lunch we had to gather them for nap time and this was a challenge because sometimes they would find a way to try to have sex with the female residents and if they weren't having sex they would go to the shower and masturbate. Seeing a mentally challenged person masturbate is a site to see - working at Caswell Center I had to encounter these types of things. If anyone tried to intervene while they were performing these acts, they had a task on your hands.

One thing we must remember is that people that are mentally challenged have sexual arousals and feelings just like everyone else.

No one wanted to be the first person to go *stop* the act, because the residents would try to beat you down. I always hated when it was a full moon, the residents that were calm all of a sudden turned wild and the residents that were already wild turned even wilder. Sometimes we would have three or four fights breaking out at the same time. When I grabbed one of them to take them down to the floor without trying to hurt them, I couldn't keep them down for long because they were slinging me off of them as soon as I took them down to the floor.

I would tell the nurse, "When I take them down again I can only hold them for about ten seconds; you should be able to give them a shot of Thorazine in those ten seconds."

After the Thorazine shot was administered the resident's movements would slow down. After all the excitement I would be drenched with sweat. There weren't too many days that I would come to work and *not work*. Believe it or not, I enjoyed working at Caswell Center.

CHAPTER 21

My Sport Career Begins

I went out for the football team and made it. The position I played was quarterback. This was not *street ball*! This was organized sports. I wanted to be like my Uncle Jay because he played quarterback.

I had a strong left arm but I didn't have the fundamentals down packed. Jay was the coach and he would let me know that I didn't have the fundamentals right.

When I ran the wrong play, Jay would embarrass the hell out of me by grabbing me by the helmet and pulling me towards him and began to fuss at me for messing the play up. I got so nervous I messed up all the plays. The guys were laughing about this.

Jay was worse than Denderant on that football field, if you messed up, Jay made sure you knew. The same man that taught me to never allow anyone to take away my confidence was the same man that took it away in football. He always had a habit of restoring my confidence when we would ride home after football practice.

It's hard playing for a relative because they expect you to not make any mistakes and they get on you extra hard because they don't want to be seen as showing favoritism.

After practice, Jay would talk to me and I would get my confidence back.

He said, "Gold, you got to be poised when you are playing quarterback because you are the leader, you can't be nervous, and you have to concentrate. I know you can get the job done. You have to stand in the pocket instead of running the ball. I didn't have any choice but to run because my line didn't block."

Needless to say I didn't get the job done because I was second string quarterback. All the games we played were away games and I saw little action.

The season was fun because I loved traveling on the bus and joking with the boys. The boys would say, "Damn, Gold you only got sixty seconds worth of action on the field. Your uniform is still clean."

Me (#5) and My Football Team, My Uncle Jay (Coach) is on the Far Right at the Back

After the football season was over it was time for basketball season. Following the basketball season, I tried out for the track team. I had never run track before so I didn't know what event to run.

Coach Little and my Uncle Jay were the track coaches. When we had to report to practice, we had to run cross country then we could start practice. I started off last and ended up last running cross country. I was never a long distant runner. It took me so long to run the cross country that the team started practice without me. My Uncle Jay decided to give me a shot at running the 400 yard dash. That is one lap around a quarter mile track.

I remember my first track meet; I asked one of my friends Jimmy Brunson, "What is the best way to run the 400?" Jimmy was the fastest man on the team and he was one of Kinston's best running back, in my opinion.

Jimmy said, "Gold this is how you run the 400 yard dash. You start off slow and when you get to the last one hundred yards, that's when you turn on your speed."

When the race started, I did like Jimmy said and when I got to the 300 yard mark I decided to turn on my speed, but the race was already over with; I came in last. I never got any more advice from Jimmy.

In the future, Jimmy and I would become good friends and we would run on relays together and set records. I ran the

400 yards in 63 seconds and that's when the coach started calling everyone who ran the 400 yard dash in over a minute, he called them minute men. Before the year was out, I got my time up under a minute; I think my best time was 58 seconds. I told the coach he can stop calling me a minute man. I really didn't like track because of my asthma but I was a sports fanatic.

In my eighth grade year I got cut from the basketball team, I didn't do well in football or track. I started to give up on playing sports with the school team and go back to playing street ball, but I gave it one more shot the next year and I never regretted it. This should be a lesson to kids never give up, no matter what you do.

CHAPTER 22

Coming into My Town

I decided to go out for the freshman basketball team. I had gotten cut the year before. I was very hesitant but I went out for the team anyway. I knew I could play basketball but Kinston breeds basketball players, everyone couldn't make the team and it wasn't because they couldn't play, but the city of Kinston had so much talent in basketball.

When you hear of Kinston, you think about basketball greats. You think about people like Cedric Maxwell, former Boston Celtics MVP in the NBA Championship, Charles Shackelford, who played with many NBA teams, and Jerry Stackhouse, who also played with several NBA teams, and is still playing. We also had our football greats that played in the National Football League, Lin Dawson and Ronald Wooten.

I remember when Langley High School came to town, this is the school Michael Jordon played with; the gym was packed. Michael Jordon used to put on a show, but he wasn't the only one putting on a basketball clinic, my cousin Herbert Suggs, my main man Vincent Lewis put on a basketball clinic as well. When Jordon came down and dunked the ball, either Vincent Lewis or Herbert would come down and dunk the ball too.

Micheal Jordan and My Buddy Vincent Lewis Goes Up For a Rebound During a Home Game at Kinston High School in Kinston, N.C.
The Home of The Mighty Vikings!!!!!!!!!!!!

The Kinston High School coach used to put his best defensive players in to defend *tongue-wagging* Michael Jordon. There were more players that should have been in the NBA from Kinston, either they didn't apply themselves or the coach didn't notify them of the college teams that were interested in them.

I remember being at a track meet and my cousin Herbert was there and the opposing track coach wanted to know where was he going to school and he said he didn't know. What Herbert didn't know was, the Kinston High basketball coach only gave him the name of the *black colleges* that was interested in him, this was a tradition with the basketball coach, and a lot of players missed great opportunities because of this coach. My cousin was able to go to Tulsa and play ball not because of his basketball coach but because of my Uncle Jay.

Uncle Jay and the eighth grade basketball coach (Little) was responsible for most of the black basketball players getting into college to play sports. I can name all the great players that came out of Kinston High School but they are too many to mention. The reason we played Michael Jordon's school twice a year was because they were in our conference.

Getting back to my basketball skills, I was quick with my hands and I practiced hard and I could play defense; Coach Hamilton was the basketball coach as well as the driver's education teacher and he would make comments when he saw me practice, good defense.

"What's your name?"

"Garry Jones."

This was a great sign when a coach wanted to know your name, this meant that they were interested or you did something good to get their attention because there were a lot of people who tried out for the team that he didn't even know or cared to know their names.

The first week went by and the basketball team had their first cut. After practice the coach said, "If I call your name this means you made the first cut and if I don't call your name, this mean that you can go home."

I think my name was the fifth name Coach Hamilton called. I was happy as hell, but it wasn't over. He cut about twenty-five players that day; he was trying to get the roster down to ten players. This left us with twenty players trying to make the team.

Coach Hamilton would constantly say, "Good defense Jones." He never said anything about my offense even though I could play with the best of them.

I played point guard and if I messed up the play, he would stop to tell me where I made my mistake. This made me think I wasn't going to make the team because I kept on running the plays wrong or someone would mess up and the point guard would be blamed for it.

Take for an example, when you know you screwed up a play, you continue with the play. You bring the basketball back out at the top of the key and start the play over, but some jackass would tell the coach I messed up, hell the coach knew that I messed up, he created the play.

This made me step up my defense game another notch; I knew the coach loved someone who could play defense. Whoever told the coach that I messed up the play, I would put that defense on them so hard that they couldn't get the ball across half court. I had the speed and quickness to do this. I even had the leaping ability to snatch a couple of rebounds and strong enough to box you out.

I remember the coach giving me a compliment for boxing players out. I was about 5'6" at the time and was able to jump high enough to touch the basketball rim. The next week the final cut came. I was nervous because I had made several mistakes. I remember the compliment the coach gave me on defense but at the same time, I remember him telling me about the mistakes I was making on offense.

Earlier, I mentioned that I was a point guard but Dalton and Alonzo had that position on lock down, I knew if I made the team, I would have to play behind those guys. After practice, the coach called us in the middle of the court and said,

"I can only keep ten players, I wish I could keep everyone but I can't. I have to let eight of you all go, not because I want to."

Butterflies were in my stomach, I thought about being cut from the team last year and how it felt. I didn't want to feel that way again.

Coach Hamilton did the same thing that he did the week prior, he said, "If I call your name that meant you made the team and if I don't, this means you have to go home while I have a meeting with the team."

There were at least eight people that I knew of that was already going to make the team. Cousin Herbert Suggs, Michael Fields, Alfonzo Jenkins, of course Dalton Frizzell (Sutton), Alonzo Rhem; the white guy Derrick Johnson and Bo Kintz; I can't think of the names of the other guys that I knew who would make the team. I knew I had a very good chance but I wasn't for sure.

When the coach started calling names, it seemed as if he took forever, the time just stopped or either it went in slow motion. The coach called the first eight names, these were the people who I knew that was already on the team because they made the team the year before and five of them started and the other three got regular playing time. When the coach got to the 9th name, he called Tony Hill (Rest in Peace); he was my best friend in Carver Courts other than Antray. When the coach got to the 10th and final name, I started sweating. Coach Hamilton called the 10th name and that name was Garry Jones aka "Goldwater" I said to myself, "Thank God!"

I really didn't want to celebrate because I knew some of the guys that didn't make the team and I felt bad for them. After the coach selected who was going to play for him , he said a few words and congratulated us on making the freshman basketball team and he told us to meet him at practice at 4 p.m. the next day. Even though I felt bad for the other ones, I ended up going home to celebrate; this may have been one of the greatest moments in my life.

Me (#5) and My Basketball Team During My Freshman Year

When the season started we all had *guardian angels*, but we never knew who they were. We knew they were cheerleaders but whom? The guardian angels would make us a food basket before every game...my guardians hooked me up!

As a matter of fact, during the whole basketball year every week I got the biggest basket with the most snacks in it.

Everyone wanted to know who my guardian angel was but we didn't find out until the end of the season.

We only lost three games during the season and I did get playing time and sometimes the coach would put me in when the other team had their best offensive player on the team. Whenever Tony Hill and I were in the game at the same time, I would pass the ball to him or either he would pass the ball to me. I used to get the ball and take it through my legs and around my back but wouldn't shoot. When I would get home later that night, my Uncle Jay would say, "Gold when you get in the game you have to shoot the ball."

I pride myself on playing good defense. My girlfriend Sherrill would be at every game and when I go in the game we would make eye contact. I wanted to make sure I did well because she was looking. I lost the ball out of bounds one time because I was too busy staring in the stand. We dated for about six months and the relationship was great. I remember walking to her house during the holidays.

I didn't have a car so I had to hit the pavement. I was weighing about one hundred pounds; whenever I would go to her house, her mother would always ask me did I want something to eat. Most of the times I said no, her family was really crazy about me. I stayed over to her house until it got dark and her mother made her oldest brother take me back home.

During the Christmas holidays, I didn't know what to get her for Christmas, so I decided to ask my Aunt Mary, "What do you get a girl for Christmas?"

"Girls love to have a necklace."

I didn't have the money to buy the necklace so my Aunt Mary brought me the necklace to give to my girlfriend for Christmas. This girl was fine as hell; she was short and had long wavy hair.

She loved the necklace and we both loved our favorite song by Barry White, "*Just the Way You Are.*" Isaac Hayes had the same song out at the same time called, "*Don't Go Changing, "I Love You Just the Way You Are.*" Our relationship would eventually break off because she didn't want to have sex, she was a virgin. She would always tease me like she was going to give me some but she never did.

After the basketball season was over I found out who my guardian angel was; her name was Sallie Davis. She made sure I had the most snacks in my bag. Sallie and I would become very good friends after that.

CHAPTER 23

Football and Track Season, 1979

The football season came around quick and yes, I was still playing quarterback. My skills had improved but not good enough to be a starter. My confidence was up but the first quarterback Bo Kintz had better poise than me, so he got the position, although I did play during the season.

Me Posing For an Individual Picture at Kinston High School

My knowledge of the position had grown a lot but the blocking still wasn't there. The line didn't block when I came into the game which forced me to run the ball a lot. This gave people the perception that all I wanted to do was run the ball which was not true.

The 1979 football season came and went and I can't remember how many games we had won. In my 9th grade year I started dating again and I met this girl, both of us fell in love quick. The only chance I had to spend time with her was at school.

Her parents didn't allow me to come to the house or should I say didn't allow me to come in the house when I came over to see her. She and I did most of our dating at school. I can recall my first kiss with her; this made me fall in love even deeper.

During exam times, me, her and a couple of more people went over to my classmate house and made love. She had on a blue Terrie cloth short outfit. We both were kind of nervous because we were virgins.

Whenever her mother would put her on punishment, I wouldn't dare come over to her house. She wasn't able to use the telephone when she was on punishment. We both got around that. I used to have my sister Lisa to call her house and after Lisa talked with her she would give the phone to me. When you are in love, you find ways of getting around things.

I knew when I walked her home, I would miss the school bus to take me home, but I didn't give a damn, after seeing her, the three mile walk to get back home was a breeze because the only thing that was on my mind when I was walking was the conversation we had just had.

I remember when Belinda and I were going to the Freshman Ball. The plan was for her mother to bring her to Kinston High School, where the Freshman Ball was being held at. I stayed across the street from Kinston High School. Belinda was supposed to walk across the street to my house and we were going to walk in as a couple. I had my corsage and my grandmother was going to show me how to pin the corsage on Belinda when she came over to the house but she never showed up.

My grandmother kept asking, "Garry, where is she?"

"I don't know."

I was embarrassed. I finally went over to the school and the first person I seen at the Freshman Ball was Belinda.

"Why didn't you come over to the house?"

"My mother wouldn't let me."

I told her, "I thought your mother had agreed to bring you over to the house."

"I thought the same thing, but she changed her mind."

It was track season again and this time, it was my breakout year. I was very good in the 400 yard dash, during the year. I only got first or second place. I was still dating my new girlfriend. We would walk each other to our lockers during the changing of class.

There was this one time when they called for the track team from over the public address system to meet at the bus for an out of town track meet; my girlfriend and I were talking at the locker, she was there to wish me luck and this other girl came up to me who used to like me and put her finger in my face and said, "Garry, why didn't you call me back last night."

I told the girl to get her fingers out of my face but she didn't and we started fighting. This girl put her fingers in the back on my neck and scratched the hell out of me; blood was coming down my neck. I was taught to never hit a girl but my instinct to protect myself came out of me. The fight was broken up by other students and we both went to the principal's office. The girl that I was fighting, her mother was a school teacher at the same school we attended. After her mother came to the office, she was told that her daughter started the fight with me and after her mother seen my neck, she took her daughter out of the office and whipped the hell out of her. She told my grandmother she would pay for the doctor bill. When I reported to the bus, my neck was burning and I could feel the blood drying up. It was hot that day. My Uncle Jay had already found out what had happen and he told me to get on the bus; he would deal with me when I got home.

Needless to say this was the first time I had gotten first place in the 400 yard dash. When the gun was fired to start the race, my neck was burning so bad that I couldn't wait to finish the race. I ran my ass off and got first place.

During My Track Star Days

After we got back from the track meet, Jay and I went home and Jay took off his belt and told my grandmother that I was fighting a girl. Before Jay could whip me, my grandmother said, "Garry doesn't mess with anyone, she must have been meddling him; he has the right to defend himself."

My grandmother saved me that day and until this day I have never fought another woman again. When I came back the school the next day, it was a tradition of the school to announce over the public address system who had came in what place at the track meet. Of course my neck was bandaged up but when they called my name for taking first place in the 400 yard dash, I was happy.

Having my girlfriend and receiving first place, I was in dream land. Jay still had a leash on me, if my grades weren't up to par. In the summer of 1979 Jay put me on punishment and made me come in the house at 9 p.m. because I failed an exam.

'Jay, I was promoted to the 10th grade and my grades were decent and plus I played basketball, football, ran track and went to the Jr. Olympics all in the same year,' is what I thought to myself.

I couldn't believe I was on punishment in the summer time, of course I didn't let the girls know I was on punishment nor did I let the fellows know. I would come up with some lame excuse like I needed to be around the house at night because of my grandmother. My grandmother was fifty-two years old; she didn't need a man around the house.

I went on to run Jr. Olympics that summer. In 1979, it was a great year because I was in love but at the same time it was a hurtful year because I lost four people that I knew very well - Vince Davis (murdered) and Curt Turnage (murdered), Rob Streeter, died of an illness, and Johnny Staten died in a car accident.

CHAPTER 24

High School

In 1980 I went off to high school and was getting into football and the rest of the sports very heavy. Belinda and I were still an item. I was playing junior varsity football, she would come to see me play - I was still playing second string quarterback and Bo was still playing first string quarterback. Before practice, Belinda and I would meet somewhere private in the school and kiss before every practice.

When game time came, I was getting more action than I had gotten the previous years but the front line was not blocking.

I remember when we had a home game and the coach told me to start warming up my arm; I guess Bo wasn't having a good game and they put me in to play, mainly because my arm was stronger than his arm. Meaning I could throw the ball further but I could never get a pass off because I was always running for my life.

Josh Wooten, who used to run the recreation center for Carver Courts noticed what was going on. He told me that whenever I would go in the game, the front line would step aside and let the defense come in on me and that is why I couldn't get a play off because before my center could hack me the ball, the defense was already in the back field. This shit was getting political now and Josh was the only one that noticed what was going on.

There came a time when I was able to get a couple of plays off. The first year Michael Fields was my fullback and Michael Pittman was my running back. Both of these guys were good. Pittman and I ran track together and Michael Fields and I grew up together.

During the time that I was able to get a play off without running, Michael Fields was so strong he was *taking the ball out of my hands*! The play that was called was for me to fake giving the ball and pitching the ball to Pittman. Kinston High always ran that option. I loved this type of offense. It gave me an option to give Fields the ball if the hole was open and if the hole wasn't open it gave me the opportunity to pitch the ball to Pittman. Sometimes the defense would get to me before I could pitch the ball to Pittman and that's when I chose to run the ball myself, actually I was *forced* to run the ball.

After the football season was over with, me and Belinda's relationship was on shaky grounds. Belinda was infatuated with the older guys. She was popular and everybody was trying to hit on her because of who her father was. We finally called it quits; actually she called it off before I knew that it was called off. Someone told me that she had already started liking this older guy. This broke my heart. This was the first time my heart had ever been broken and being with another woman was never the same because I started breaking their hearts. I had given up on playing basketball and concentrated on playing football and running track.

My 11th grade year had come around and I had already become a track star. I was in all the relays and from time to time I ran the 100 and the 200 yard dash. Kinston High Track team was loaded with talent. Fortunate enough I was an asset to every relay team.

Track Team, First Row Center – Me, First Row Far Right End – Uncle Jay

Of course I was taking off some relay teams to run individual events. When you run track, you could only participate in three running events and one field event. The school had a new track field and the fans were coming out to see the track team. Track had gotten just as exciting as football and basketball.

When football season came back around I was still playing quarterback; still playing behind Bo Kinzt. My running back was Capp and I forgot who my full back was. I remember playing against Langley High School, the school Michael Jordan was attending.

The starting quarterback was Bo Kintz, Bo had gotten hurt and the varsity coach just happened to be at the game. The coach called me to go in the game to replace Bo. The play was a Green 23 option; the play was designed to fake giving the football to the full back and pitch the ball to the running back. The team we were playing had already figured out how to stop the option. They had someone spying on the fullback, quarterback, and the running back.

When the play started, I couldn't fake giving the ball to the full back because the defense was already in my backfield, so when I tried to pitch the ball to Capp, someone was already going towards Capp and if I would have pitched the ball to

Capp he would have lost yardage so I tucked the ball away and ran for thirty yards.

When I went back in the huddle to call another play I turned and saw Bo hopping back on the field, he said, "Gold, I came back to replace you."

I went to the sidelines and ask the coach, "What in the hell did I do wrong!"

"You did well."

"Well why did you take me out of the game?"

He never answered my question. One of my friends Jeff Jenkins who was on the team called me to the bench and said that he heard the varsity coach tell the J.V. coach to get me out of the damn game. He didn't want a running quarterback. I said to myself, f- him, he is the varsity coach, why is he controlling what the junior varsity team is doing.

The next day in practice, the junior varsity coach told me that he was changing my position to wide receiver, I couldn't play quarterback anymore and I said I quit the team. Football was my first love and track was something I was good at but I didn't love it.

I was still into the women; one of my friend's named Capp said this girl named Shirley liked me and wanted to talk to me but Capp was lying. When I spoke to Shirley she showed no interest. I told Capp that he lied and Shirley didn't like me and that's when Capp said, "Gold, I bet you can't get her to like you because she doesn't like under classman."

"If I really wanted her I could pull her!"

After I started to talk with Shirley we began to like each other but she was involved with this marine but I kept after Shirley and eventually we started dating. I had a lot of feelings for Shirley but not playing football was heavy on my mind.

The junior varsity coach came over to my house and told me he wanted me to come back on the team but I couldn't play quarterback, this was not his decision, it was the varsity coach decision. I gave in because football was my first love.

When I came back to the team, I wasn't starting at wide receiver and I wasn't crazy about this. I had to earn the position. During the next game I did earn the position because the coach put me in the game and I scored a 50 yard touchdown pass the first time I touched the field. I started the rest of the season.

Shirley and I started dating real heavy and the holidays were coming in. I used to tell Shirley about my dreams of becoming a professional boxer. One Christmas Shirley brought me some boxing gloves. When I opened my gift I was excited, I took my gift home and showed it to Jay; Jay started joking and Capp just happened to be over at the house that day. Jay told Capp what kind of woman would buy her boyfriend some boxing gloves. Capp said, "She must want him to go up side her head."

Jay killed himself laughing. Shirley and I dated for about a year and her family was crazy about me. I couldn't do any wrong in their eyes. My family was crazy about Shirley; as a matter of fact my family loved all of my girlfriends I brought over to the house.

Going into my senior year, I was still playing football; we had a new coach with these strict rules, he was a politician. In the summertime most black players had to work and they couldn't get summer practice in the morning but they made the evening practice.

They also didn't have cars so they had to catch a ride to practice. Most white players had their own cars. This new coach wanted to kick them off the team; he wanted to know what was more important, working or coming to practice. He never took into consideration that some parents made their children work during the summer.

I was blessed to not have to work during the summer so I came to summer practice but I still had to catch a ride. I was a great wide receiver but I didn't start in my senior year, a junior started in front of me and I believe the coach let him start because his father worked for the Kinston board of education. This guy didn't have the talent I had. It was politics not racism because the guy who started in front of me was black.

It didn't last long because after the second game I was starting at wide receiver.

My relationship with Shirley began to dissipate and we would eventually break up. I ran one more season of track and I got better and better. A lot of colleges were trying to recruit me. I'm not bragging but I was a track superstar and the whole Kinston knew about it but the love for track still wasn't in my heart.

Women and football was my appetite. I remember going to hang out on the block in Carver Courts; a guy named Turner was on the block and he wanted to race me, he was an older guy. He was supposed to be fast but he had the nerve to want to race me in the streets. Another homeboy name Yogi told Turner not to race me, as a matter of fact; Yogi put his money on me. I didn't have the money to bet Turner but I knew I could whip him in running.

Turner and I got in the middle of the streets by First Missionary Baptist Church and took off running, after the first

ten yards, I smoked Turner and looked back at him and started laughing…Yogi won his money and I left the block.

CHAPTER 25

Heading to North Carolina Central University

I awakened one Sunday morning and the phone rang; Jay was on the other end, "Gold you ready?"

"Yes, I will be ready shortly."

I was ready to leave home but when the time came for me to go to college I had butterflies in my stomach. It wasn't like I was going somewhere I didn't know people, but being away from home on my own was something I had to get used to.

Jay and his wife Debra came by to pick me up to take me to the famous North Carolina Central University, two hours away from my hometown. Debra was an alunmi of N.C.C.U. as well. We left Kinston and then we stopped by Raleigh, N.C. to pick up my *other mother* Mavis, she is my aunt but most people call her my mother sometimes because she is always taking care of me.

She took on the responsibility of looking out for me since I was going to college, I had a *nice* mother named Mavis and a *mean* mother named Denderant - both were my aunts. After picking up Mavis, we headed thirty miles away to NCCU, the home of the Eagles that fly high and look low.

After we arrived, I said, 'So this is where I'm going to be.' In my heart I said, 'I don't have any intentions on staying at this school, do I really want to go to school or what, or should I have gone into the military.'

My mind was going backwards and forward. I'm a grown man now and I am responsible for every decision I make whether it be good or bad.

When I arrived it was alright, but when they left and when I waved good bye, it wasn't a party, I felt empty inside. I went to the front lobby to pick up my room key. I said to myself, 'I am actually on my own.' I had money in my pocket and a lot of high school books that I could look at, yearbooks and stuff like that.

I went to my room, and one of my home boys named Derrick Moore and my cousin John Grimes (Style Pooh) came and knocked on the door, "Come and go on the yard."

They knew it was my first time being away from home to be on my own. They were seniors. They sensed that I was feeling bad; I was feeling bad because I missed home but I was feeling happy because I was away from home. I had mixed feelings.

I left a support system…I left a program…home. What I mean by program is when you are home you are programmed to do what your people tell you to do.

That's just the bottom line. They tell you when to wake up, what to do, you need to go out there and get a job, empty the trash…such, such, such. I didn't have that anymore, which was good, but I was surrounded by brand new people, from all over the world. I left Tessie, Jay…I was glad that I left but in a sense I kind of wish they were there, I was hurt.

Shortly after or before I graduated from high school, I started dating this girl name Darlene. Then I broke it off because I didn't want a girlfriend. I wanted to be single and anyway Darlene was still in high school and in order for me to concentrate on school I needed to have my mind free.

When Jay and my two aunts got in the car to go back home I grew up quick. Derrick, John (Cousin Style Pooh), and I went on the yard and it was a different world. All of these damn women on this campus, I damn near went crazy. You meet different girls from all over the world, not just from a local city…a lot of international students at North Carolina Central University…it was sort of like Central was the main stream…Kinston was local. I was meeting people from different walks of life that were sort of like fun and exciting.

After I left the yard and returned to my room, another homeboy came over named Michael Patrick; his room was located across the hall from me. Mike said, "Where is your roommate."

"I don't think I have a roommate."

We talked a little while then Mike went back to his room. I went to sleep and shortly after that, I heard someone with a key coming into my room, the guy said, "Get the fuck up."

This guy was about 6' 10" and played on the basketball team named Doug Taylor. He had his own apartment, but he also had a key to the room. He knew he had a roommate and he also knew he was supposed to stay on campus because he was an athlete; he was on a scholarship and athletes are supposed to stay on the yard.

"I just want to see how you were," he said. "You're a big m.f. aren't you?"

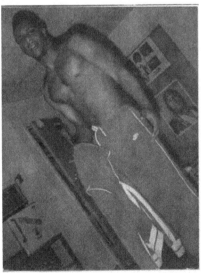

In My Room at College

I was still 135/140 pounds but I was big and cut up.

"Yeah you look like you pump those weights...tell me about yourself, I'm Doug."

He had a breathing problem just like I did, every time he spoke, he talked out of his nose.

He said, "Man I am just here and if anybody asked where I stay...I stay here. If the coach comes by you just tell them I am not here, but I stay here."

In all actuality he wanted me to lie for him.

He said, "Anything you need you let me know, I'll pick it up."

He picked me up and took me to his other place.

"What's in this refrigerator is mine...you buy shit I'm going to eat it, if I buy shit you can eat it. Oh, and I know about your homeboys."

Doug used to take me over to his house; we used to chill out and talk. I started talking about how I was a Super Star in High school, and how I would have been a Super Star in track here at Central, because they really didn't have that many people running track at North Carolina Central, as far as a sprinter.

I probably was the best sprinter out there besides Clarke who would eventually go on to play with the Detroit Lions. Doug asked me, "Are you going to go out for the track team?"

"Yes, I am going to go out."

The real reason I really didn't get into that track team is because Kinston High had more than North Carolina Central had as far as track, better facilities. Being in college you are thinking that you are going to have the best of the best then you get to college and realize you don't have shit. I had to prove myself to this new coach; I forgot the coach's name, we didn't actually get along even though I had talent.

It wasn't like I thought it was going to be…becoming a track star. I thought I was going to have better facilities and I realized Central really only had a couple of guys coming out for track.

They didn't even have enough people to put together a serious track team and I was disappointed. This is a college and when you make the team, they provide you with *something*. Hell the coach wanted us to catch a ride with the kids that had cars to run at the University of North Carolina. I couldn't believe this!

I figured if you are on a track team that meant they are supposed to provide different things for you...a couple of guys had cars and you had to get in with them to go over there. I was thinking being at college things would be more organized. I thought they had money allocated for the track team, and that there would be a van or something.

I thought we would be able to get track shoes and stuff; we wouldn't have to pay for it like we did in high school because we are on the team. I really don't think North Carolina Central had the money.

That program really went down, because they were known for their track team when Dr. Walker used to be there. This track team didn't carry over that well, then I said, "I'm not running for free" and the coach felt like, 'you haven't proved anything to me'.

One of my friends Frank Albert went to University of North Carolina (I had a scholarship offer from University of North Carolina too but I chose not to go). I went over to their college for a track meet just to see what Central had.

Mr. Little, a track coach and 8th grade basketball coach and Jay (my uncle) the assistant track coach also came up to see the college track meet. I had to catch a ride with someone else and I wasn't running for Central.

When I went over there - I specifically remember it being a Saturday - North Carolina Central coach was over there too. Hershel Walker was there running for the University of Georgia and Kevin Bryant was running for the University of North Carolina.

I remember Kevin Bryant very well because he and my homeboy Ricky White were the fastest sprinters in North Carolina in high school. Kevin went on to play with the

Washington Redskins. The North Carolina Central coach and my Uncle Jay had a talk.

Jay said, "My nephew isn't going to run for free. He doesn't have to prove his credentials, you can look at his record and tell his credentials are good and he is a track star. You are not going to get him on that team and make him do this and do that; you're going to provide him with something or he is not going to run for you."

Me, Passing Baton in 400 Meter Relay

Eventually Jay said, "He isn't going to run at all."

Of course, I said, "I am going to do what Jay say do...I'm not going to run."

I wasn't impressed with the coach anyway, that was sort of my excuse not to be able to run. Like I said earlier, my high school provided for us in track better than NCCU.

I'm not putting my school down because they are truly awesome *now*!!!! It's just that track was not number one on the list of sports that the school put money into when I attended college. They weren't providing me with anything, if I am a superstar you got to provide me with things like my track shoes.

On the other, hand in a way I understood what the coach was saying, 'You got to prove something to me,' but I had displayed all of the credentials out there for the coach to see – the things I did in high school.

All of this took place in the fall. We had to practice in October to compete in indoor track. It was only a few months before trying out for the Central team that I was participating in the High School State Track meet. I did all of this in May '82, we went out there and broke records. I say 'we' because I was on the team that broke records 800 meter relay team and 400 meter relay team that broke records, new records.

This was just in the month of May, now we are talking about the fall (August). I hadn't lost that much ability; the new coach knew I had a potential to become a super star at Central. I didn't have any problems running track for North Carolina Central and I didn't have any problems being groomed by the coach, but damn provide me with something. Needless to say I never ran track for North Carolina Central University.

Speaking of playing sports, Mike Patrick said, "Hey man why don't you go out for the football team?"

"Why don't you go out for the *baseball* team, hell you were good in high school as a matter of fact you were a superstar."

"But you can run though, and we need someone from Kinston to represent us in sports," Mike said.

The fellows really wanted to see me make it because they had gotten into the women; sports weren't on their mind. I was a freshman and they knew I had talent, the same talent they had when they got to school but they didn't take the advantage of it. They knew if I made the football team, girls would come, not because you were a superstar, but just the fact that you were *on the team.*

Sports attracted women and if a homeboy is playing they could pick whatever woman they liked because the groupies love guys who played sports.

After Doug and I had that long talk, the next day I went on campus to register for my classes. The lines were very long. I started to get out of line and say, "Forget college!"

This is the hardest thing you have to do in college is to register for those classes. I should have come to school a week early to register for my classes because you could take advantage of what classes you wanted. I learned real fast that the classes that I had registered for were filled. It literally took a whole day to get the classes I wanted and to make sure my grant was valid.

I seen a lot of people who had to go home and come back the next semester because they didn't have a grant or their grant money was screwed up. Thank God that when I finally got in the financial aide office, my name was on the register and there weren't any problems with my grant. I have to thank my Aunt Denderant for that because she filled out all of my paperwork in high school.

After I finished registering, I ran into Michael again and he said, "Man, let's go down to Churches Chicken on Fayetteville Street and get three wings and a biscuit for a dollar."

Those wings were the biggest wings I had ever had, those wings must have had steroids in them but they were good. After eating we hooked up with Pooh and Moe and they introduced me to a couple of ladies and the rest is history. I didn't need anyone to tell me how to talk to a woman. The only thing you had to do was introduce me and I would take it from there. Sometimes if I was interested in a woman I would introduce myself to them.

After I left the fellows, I went back to the room, the lonely feeling hit me again. If I wanted to make a phone call I had to go in the hallway to wait in line to make a collect call. It's amazing when you go off to college, how you start missing the little bitty things that you were used to having; things like picking up a phone and calling whoever you wanted, taking a shower in private, looking at T.V. by yourself, and kicking it with your homeboys, like Antray and Capp.

It didn't take long for me to get a T.V.; I wasn't going to the lobby everyday just to watch T.V. As far as friends were concerned I was forced to make new friends. One of my best friends named Antray was still in my hometown and my other best friend, Capp, was attending Fayetteville State University. Capp always had a way to make things work to your benefit.

Capp would contact me with a calling card number and I would use that calling card number to call long distance although within a few days the company would catch on to the fact that someone was using their calling card without permission and they would cancel the card.

Two days later, Capp would call me again with a new calling card number and I would use it as much as possible until it was terminated. This went on for two years. One day this girl name Lula told me that the FBI called her house and asked her if she knew or spoke with anyone at North Carolina Central University, she told them, 'No.'

I guess she got scared and told them she didn't know what they were talking about. The FBI had caught on to this calling card scheme and they were narrowing it down to catch the people who were using these calling cards. I remember Capp calling me and telling me that the FBI came and got him out of class and took him and questioned him asking him if he knew anyone from North Carolina Central University that he calls, he told them, 'No.' The FBI was getting close, but the people I knew didn't snitch.

One day in my criminal justice class my instructor said, "I want to talk to you. The FBI wanted to know if I had a Garry

Jones in my class. I told them 'yes.' They also asked me how you were as a student. I told them, that you are a good student. I don't know what you have gotten yourself into, but you need to quit."

The instructor told them 'when' I would be attending class again, so I chilled from going to class for a few days, the FBI was waiting but nothing ever happened after that.

CHAPTER 26

Falling in Love Again

Me a Few Years Later After Getting Into Weightlifting

I am going to be candid with you...I started building myself up, really getting into the weights 'because I had a surprise for everybody I wasn't going to run track, I was going to try out for the football team like Michael Patrick suggested.

In November '83 is when I was pumping weights and thinking about trying out for this football team. I had met several females on Campus but it was nothing like I was interested in...yeah, I did a few things with those women, but I just wasn't in love with them.

In December of 1983 I started talking with this female from my hometown when I was home for the holidays. Me and this female was intimate one time when I was in high school, this was right after she had gotten mad with her boyfriend and she called herself getting him back by being intimate with me.

Around Christmas time the relationship had gotten a little more serious. She had just broken up with her boyfriend for many years and we started our relationship even though she still had feelings for her former boyfriend. I began to fall in love with her, when January of 1984 came around I was still lifting weights and going home every weekend until I fell in love with Barbara.

She had a son already; he was about three years old, he didn't accept me right away because he was crazy about his father but his father would never spend time with him. His father would call and tell Barbara to have Derrick ready to be picked up on the weekends but his father would never show up or call.

Young Derrick

I can see Derrick right now and how he used to be at the door waiting for his father and when someone knocked on the door he would be very excited but when I would look on his face, I saw disappointment. This kid was hurt.

This went on for a couple of months until Derrick stopped believing in his father but he still didn't accept me. I don't care what I would do, he wasn't accepting me; I would read him bedtime stories before I went to bed but even with this I could tell he wasn't really in tune to me. I understood, to him I was a stranger. Eventually he started to open up.

Being that it was New Year's (January), my mind set was to still train and try out for North Carolina Central football team. Each month would pass by and I was falling deeper and deeper for this woman. When spring of 1984 came around, I had to make a decision either go out for the football team or just continue to come home every weekend.

I knew if I made the football team, I couldn't come home every weekend because I had to practice and go off to play games. The decision came easy, the hell with football, I couldn't stand being away from my girlfriend. I was *whipped* and didn't care. The fact that I didn't play sports, school didn't appeal to me; my attention was on my girlfriend and making money.

I stopped going to class and my grades began to drop, I had made up my mind that I was going in the military and eventually get married. I remember going home and taking the army test, the guy asked me about my health and I told him I had asthma and he said it probably wasn't a good idea to go in the military because I wouldn't make it through basic training. I told him I'm used to asthma and I played sports all of my life.

I took his advice and didn't apply, but my grades had already dropped meaning that I received a letter at home about being on academic probation and if I didn't bring my grades up I would be suspended for a semester.

I remember being at home when I got the letter; I knew what was in the letter so I hid it. I think my grades had dropped to a 1.9 and when your grade point average dropped that low, it takes a long time to bring that grade point average up.

I knew I couldn't afford to make anything less than a C to at least bring the grade point average up to a 2.5. I was in trouble and I knew it. I went to summer school to bring my grades up. I knew it was important to go ahead and decide what I would be majoring in because after summer school I was going into the fall as a junior. I had a pretty good idea what I would be majoring in but it wasn't a definite thing.

Going into my junior year I knew my grades had to start improving if I wanted to graduate on time. I knew I had to start busting my ass in school because I came to a conclusion in my mind that majoring in criminal justice was best for me because every time I took a criminal justice course I enjoyed it.

I was an average student, I can't recall buying too many books while I was in school, I may have bought one or two books during the time I was in school; do you know what I used to do? I made sure I went to school everyday and didn't miss any classes, I made sure I listened 'real good' because I knew I didn't have any books, I just took notes.

One weekend I went home and asked my father could he give me some money for my books I said, "Man I need some money to buy a book, you know, my school books."

"Man I don't have g-damn money, ask your damn mama"…

My mama didn't have any money to send me to purchase my books, I just said, 'forget it, I won't get any books, I'll continue to do like I had been doing, not buy any books.'

I could tell my father felt like I was irresponsible because he had already given me a car and someone stole the car, he thought that it was one of my friends that used to ride in my car. He felt like I let someone drive the car and they made a key and stole the car and to top it off, my daughter Latoya was born and I was still in school and I had no way of supporting her.

I said to myself, 'This guy got some money, it's not like I'm asking for money to buy any drugs or alcohol.' I knew in order to go into my junior year I needed some books because my grades were down.

Eventually I would have to start buying some books. Sometimes my father can go into left field when you ask him for some money, he turns into another person.

I was depressed and now I had a child and didn't have money for books. My V.A. check hadn't come in when the fall quarter started and I needed money for books. I said forget it.

Needless to say I went back to school without the money for books. Another reason I didn't have any money is because I was staying in an apartment; bills had to be paid, but having a child was my responsibility; 'I brought this child into this world and it is my responsibility to raise the child and if a relative doesn't help then I can't get mad at them.'

I decided to continue to pass the old fashioned way, I went to class and took notes; that's how I passed college, by taking notes. I had *access* to the money, but I just couldn't keep on asking my family. Colleen (Mavis) would have stepped up to the plate like she always do, but I didn't ask.

I was determined I wasn't going to ask her. Colleen sent me money all the time but I didn't buy any books. The highest you can get, when you don't have a book, is probably a B or a C. But sometimes when instructors teach, they don't just teach everything by the notes; there are certain things in that book that you are going to have to *read* that they are not going to go over.

I went to summer school and took a couple of Criminal Justice Courses and made 2 B's. Then the next Semester I made an A, 2 B's and a C and 1 D; that kind of hurt, because I couldn't afford to make a D.

I didn't have the books but I was still rolling...just imagine if I had the books. On second thought even if I had the books my grades still could have been the same; just because you have books doesn't guarantee you an A. To be honest with you, in retrospect, the reason I didn't want to buy a book is because some of the things were hard for me to comprehend.

I just hated spending forty or fifty dollars on a book trying to read something I didn't comprehend. To be able to comprehend early in life...you got to get in the habit of reading. Jay always preached that to me, "Gold you have to read all the time." Every now and then I would borrow someone's book to read and give it back to them.

Today, it bothers me that I was so blinded by love. I think I could have been a potential superstar and I allowed love to stop me from pursuing my football dreams. I knew I could have been a superstar in track but the passion wasn't there.

I never got into the athletic world the way I wanted to, I didn't even scratch the surface. The thing I enjoyed most about my college experience was being away from home; being able to drink, and go to parties. It was the end of my sophomore year and it was time to get serious and find out what I wanted to major in. You really don't get serious into your education until you are a junior.

You needed to already have a major in mind and work towards that goal. Your first two years you really don't know what you want to major in. I was confused...

I ended up saying, "I am going to major in Business because I heard other people say they were going to major in Business."

CHAPTER 27

He Crossed the Line

Prior to me going back to school for the fall semester in the summer of 1984 I went to visit my girlfriend one more time. It was the summer of 1984 and my girlfriend started facing financial problems; she got laid off her job. She had a gold Honda accord stick shift that she'd taught me how to drive, but the car was being threatened to be repossessed.

I was working at Nova Center for my summer job and I would ensure that I gave my grandmother her share of my paycheck even though I wasn't staying with her during the summer.

Of course I would go by the house everyday and eat her good cooking and when I would get mad at my girlfriend, I could always go back home. I would go home in the middle of the night and fall the sleep on the couch and the next morning, when I awakened a blanket would be over me and I could smell that good ole fashioned bacon, grits and eggs.

My grandmother would say, "Garry, breakfast is ready," and I would say, "I will be in the kitchen in a minute."

Every dime I gave to my grandmother, I never regretted. My grandmother would bend over backwards to ensure I had everything I needed. I can tell she wasn't comfortable with me cohabitating (shacking). During that time I felt as though I was grown but in my grandmother's eyes, I was never grown.

After giving my grandmother a portion of my paycheck, I tried to help my girlfriend with her bills. I really didn't want her car to be repossessed because I was driving that car to work most of the time.

One summer afternoon, my girlfriend left the apartment and said, "I'm going downtown to try to borrow some money at this financial company."

I told her, "If you do borrow some money from them, it's going to take forever to pay them back because they have the highest interest rates in the world."

My girlfriend was never lazy; she had always been independent, as a matter of fact I never dated a woman who was dependent on me. She was excited about going to borrow the money. One thing about a finance company, you may have bad credit but they would lend you the money and when you finish paying the loan, you would have paid the loan at least five times over. An hour later she walked back in the house without a smile on her face.

"How did it go, did you get the loan?"

"No, I didn't get the loan."

Of course she had been turned down for a loan before, but this time her demeanor was different. Normally when she would get turned down from a loan it wouldn't bother her, but I could tell something was wrong, she was holding something inside that she didn't want to tell me. She knew I was about half crazy, so therefore, she couldn't share everything with me. I insisted on asking her what happened downtown at the loan office.

"Garry, I don't want to discuss it."

"Woman what the hell you mean you don't want to discuss it!" I asked angrily. "Tell me what in the hell happened at the loan office!"

"Garry if I tell you, promise me that you are not going to snap."

"What am I going to snap over? I'm calm, now tell me what the fuck happened before I snap on your ass."

"See, you are already getting mad before I can tell you what happened."

"I wouldn't be getting mad if you would have came out and told me what happened, your ass is beating round the damn bush."

"Garry, the man said I could be approved for the loan if I came back at 5 p.m. after the office was empty and went to bed with him."

"What did you just say!"

"Garry, you said you weren't going to snap."

"Come on let's go, get the damn keys and let's get the hell out of here! Take Derrick over to your mothers house and let's go back downtown to the loan office, I'm getting ready to straighten this old bastard out!"

"I'm not going anywhere with you, if you want to go downtown, you are going to have to go by yourself."

"Oh hell no, you are going if I have to snatch your ass and put you in the car, you are going!"

She could tell by the second I was getting angrier and I had lost control. I grabbed the keys and told Derrick to get ready because he was going over to his grandmother's house and me and his mother was going down town to take care of some business.

She knew I couldn't drive the stick shift that good and she knew I didn't like to drive in traffic with the stick shift but I was so mad that I didn't give a damn if the car cut off every second. I was determined to go downtown. We dropped Derrick off to his grandmother's house and we proceeded to go downtown. She refused to drive but I didn't care; the car continued to cut off as we were leaving.

While on the way we were arguing back and forth.

"If it's not bothering me, why is it bothering you."

"Look woman you just don't let anyone disrespect you like that and get away with it!"

"I knew I shouldn't have told your stupid ass anything, Men are going to be men and you shouldn't let that bother you! You are burning my clutch, you need to change gears!"

"Don't tell me how to drive this damn car!"

"The car is going to be torn up by the time you get down town!"

"The hell with what you are talking about and don't try to change the subject. White people think they can talk to black women anyway they want to and the black women always ignore it! This is not slavery and you are *my woman* and no one is going to disrespect you. If you don't stand for something you will fall for anything!"

As we approached the loan company, I found a parking space but I had to parallel park and that is hard when you are not used to driving a stick shift.

I said the hell with the parallel parking; I will just find a parking space that I can just drive into without having to keeping on shifting gears. When I parked the car, she refused to get out of the car, I said, "If you don't get out of this car I'm going to snatch your ass out!"

She agreed to get out of the car. When we went inside the loan company, I seen my home girl in the corner typing, she was working for the loan company. When my girlfriend and I approached the desk where the loan officer was, this white old man came out and said, "Oh, you are back again."

He had a smile on his face when he was talking with my girlfriend. I informed the loan officer that I was the boyfriend and my girlfriend said that you said she could get the loan if she came back at 5 p.m. and had sex with you.

"Sir, this must have been a mistake I would never say anything like that."

I grabbed that loan officer by his neck tie and brought him closer to me and told him that he was lying and if he didn't apologize to my girlfriend, I would break his damn neck; that man turned redder than blood. I refused to let him go because I was still mad, he apologized and my girlfriend said, "Garry let him go!"

While still holding the man by his tie, I told him that my grandfather was the President of the NAACP chapter of Kinston, and he is the Vice President of the NAACP chapter for the state of North Carolina and I would have that financial office closed down.

After I let the man go, my girlfriend and I left. I told her we were going to the police station to file a report. She was reluctant, believing that his apology was sufficient. I didn't care about his being *sorry* he was going to pay for his conduct,

She wanted me to just leave the situation alone and return home; I was not leaving anything alone. When I spoke to the captain of the police department and informed him of what had happened, he stated that he can charge the loan officer for solicitation.

The captain said, "I want your girlfriend to wear a wire and when she goes back in the office for the loan; we can trap him."

I said, "I don't think that man is going to fall for that; I've already told him what I was going to do to him if this shit happens again."

The captain said, "You should have let us handle this situation, we could have gotten him."

We left the police station and argued all the way back to the apartment. We were still behind on the car payment and we didn't want repossession on her credit. One of the guys in the neighborhood had heard about Barbara trying to get rid of her car, he heard about this through my girlfriend's brother.

He came by the apartment and said he wanted to put $500 down on the car and take up payments. He said he was going to the beach with his fiancée and he would have the money the next week. We agreed that this was the right thing to do.

Later on that evening while looking at the news, a special report came across the news "Man Drowns at Beach" coming up after the commercial. When the news came back on, I recognized my home girl being interviewed. She was crying and said her and her fiancée was in the water at the beach and when she turned around she couldn't find him anymore, he went under the water and never came back up, he got caught in a current.

The man that drowned was the same man me and my girlfriend agreed to sell the car to. This was a tragic story, the car was repossessed but my home girl will have to live with her fiancée drowning for the rest of her life.

CHAPTER 28

The Classic

It was the summer of 1984 when I first moved into my apartment while attending North Carolina Central University. I needed transportation and I would always ask my father could I have one of his cars; the car I wanted was the 1965 Buick Convertible he had. My father wouldn't drive this car unless it was on the weekends; mainly Saturdays.

He would have his dog (Doberman Pincher) riding on the hood of the car just cruising around Kinston. I had told him a year ago that I wanted this car but he just shrugged me off by saying you can't handle this car. I would always say, 'Yes I can.' Anyone who knew my father knew that my father drove a hard bargain.

He wasn't going to give you anything but the people who knew me knew that I wasn't going to stop until I got what I wanted. I think this was the first time my father had ever given in to me, when I wanted something. I worried him like crazy.

One day he called me up and said come get the car. Of course when I got the car I had to hear a sermon from my father, sometimes I think he missed his calling. He should have been a preacher as many sermons as he would give.

"Goldwater, I don't want you having a lot of people riding in this car."

"Ok, I understand. Could you give me the keys?" I wanted those keys bad.

"Hold up Goldwater; let me tell you more about this car before you go jumping in it."

He could tell I was excited. After going over a few details about the car he finally handed it over. To be honest the only thing I wanted to know about the car was how you let the convertible back. I had already envisioned what I was going to do.

My mind didn't think about the mechanics of a car, I guess because my father was a mechanic, everything would have already been taking care of and it was. As long as the car crank, that was the only concern that I had. I had a lot of good times in the classic.

1965 Buick Convertible

Me and Pete on His Car – Classic in the Background

I used to go up and down on the highway; back and forth to Kinston from Durham, N.C. When I would come home to see my girlfriend, I would leave late going back to college on that Sunday. My Aunt Mavis always advised me to leave early in returning to school in case the car broke down on the highway when it was dark. I didn't think my car could break down; I had the best mechanic in the world that worked on it - my father.

The average person that looked at my car would say that car is old and the first thing that crossed their mind was, 'I wouldn't take it out of town.'

When it was getting dark, my Aunt Mavis would tell my grandmother, "You need to make Garry get on the highway, it's getting dark and he don't need to be on the highway."

I think what my Aunt Mavis told my grandmother fell on deaf ears because my grandmother didn't say anything to me. I was a grown man and I could make my own decisions; I would never disrespect my aunt in anyway possible. But, I must say my grandmother was a good listener and didn't always say what her children wanted her to say to her grandchildren. I miss her very much!

CHAPTER 29

Classic Memories

I guess you are all wondering why I called my car, *The Classic*. I can't remember who named the car The Classic; it may have been my friends, Poonie, Antray or Capp. I do know that my father said after twenty years your car becomes a classic and after twenty-five or thirty years your car is considered an antique.

But nevertheless, the name of my car was called, *The Classic*. The classic had some very exciting moments in some very exciting towns with some very exciting people riding in it. I can recall one classic memory. My homeboy, Delmus Brown (Poonie) came to see me at North Carolina Central; he stayed with a friend of his family in Durham for a couple of months. In reality, he stayed in my room on campus more than he stayed with his brother.

He got a job in Durham working in an upscale restaurant named, *Alexander*. Most of the people that came to eat in there were rich people. I remember Poonie telling me that the hamburgers in that place was some ridiculous price like $25 and the uniforms they had to wear were a black tie, white shirt and a blazer.

Whenever I didn't have money for gas, Poonie would take out his tip money and supply the classic with gas. Sometimes Poonie would bring back $75 in one night from his tips.

One day when Poonie came from work, he wanted to go over to the University of North Carolina to party. I told him that I couldn't make it, he said, "Chuck I got the money for the gas." For some strange reason, he decided to start calling me Chuck. As a matter of fact we both started calling each other Chuck from time to time.

"It's not that I don't want to go but I have a term paper I have to turn in by tomorrow in Psychology."

"Where is your book?" Poonie said.

"It's in the corner."

Poonie got the book and turned to the chapter that I was supposed to be studying to write the term paper. He got a tablet and an ink pen and within 45 minutes the paper was finished.

Within an hour we were on our way to the University of North Carolina in Chapel Hill to get our party on. We had another homeboy named Gerald that road with us to Carolina. He provided the drinks and the weed and before you knew it, we were on Country Club road trying to find Great Hall on the University of North Carolina campus where the college people party.

I didn't smoke weed that much because it made me paranoid; I didn't like putting anything in my body that made me paranoid. I *did* drink the hell out of some Cognac called *Courvoisier* and when we got to the party we were already high. We had a great time in a great city.

When we arrived back to North Carolina Central, I took a shower and got ready to go to class the next morning. My first class was Psychology; I turned in my term paper and a couple of days later my instructor returned my term paper back to me with an A; I was happy!

By this time of the year it was close to North Carolina Central's Homecoming. Normally, I had friends from Kinston and friends from other universities joining in the festivities.

I can recall one of my friends named Kelvin Edmonson (Capp) coming in town for the homecoming. He'd caught a ride from Fayetteville State University; I told him I would take him back that Sunday after homecoming, he was down.

When Sunday came around I told Capp that I wanted to leave in the afternoon to take him back to Fayetteville State University located in Fayetteville, North Carolina because I wanted to be back in Durham to attend class Monday morning.

Fayetteville State University was only an hour and a half away. Me, Poonie, and Capp got up Sunday afternoon and helped Capp put his luggage in the car and we went to the gas station to fill up the classic heading off on one of the craziest times I ever experienced in the classic.

"Capp you can drive because I need to sit in the back and study for a test," I said.

We had gotten about forty-five minutes outside of Durham, North Carolina when we heard a loud noise; Capp almost lost control of the car! I didn't know what was going on, Capp pulled to the side and we realized we had a blow out. We changed the tire and headed on our way to Fayetteville and then fifteen minutes later we heard another loud noise and I said not another blowout!!

We knew we were in trouble then because we didn't have another tire and like always little or no money. We were in the city of Fuquay Varina. It was kind of warm this particular day and we knew we would some how get some help. We sat in the car and joked a little while and then the sun started going down. Most of all the businesses were closed.

There was some wine under the driver's seat of my car; the wine was in the car from the time my father first handed it over to me. We got thirsty and drank the dinner wine. We realized we needed some help soon.

A woman stopped by, "What's wrong?"

"We have two tire blowouts and we need a tire and a rim to put on the car."

"Are ya'll college students?"

"Yes."

"Do you have any money for a tire and rim because this could be pricey?"

"We have $15."

"That is not going to be enough. Wait here until I return; I am going to find someone to help."

We got in the car; it was getting darker and it started getting cold. Twenty minutes later this lady came back with a man named, Pork Chop.

"Pork Chop, these were the students I was telling you about; they only have $15. Now, what can you do to help these students because they need to be back in school by tomorrow morning?"

Pork Chop looked at the size of the tires and said, "Since they only have $15, I will have to go to a junk yard I know and try to find a tire and a rim to fit their car. Let me see what I can do."

"I'll stay with the students until you get back."

"O'K."

We started small talk with the lady and about an hour later, Pork Chop came back with a tire and a rim. We all started smiling because we knew God had answered our prayers. We gave Pork Chop the $15 and told them that we appreciated what they had done for us and we would be back and find them when we got straight to pay them the rest of the money for helping us.

The lady said, "You don't owe us anything. You all drive safe and keep your grades up."

Me, Poonie and Capp finally made it to Fayetteville, N.C. Capp told me to stop at Churches Chicken so he could use the bathroom.

"I need to use the bathroom too."

When Capp and I came out of the restroom, Poonie was in line ordering a couple of pieces of chicken and two biscuits.

"Poonie, where you get money from?"

"Out of my socks."

"What do you mean you got money from out of your socks?"

"I always keep money in case of hard times."

I said, "We could have given that money to Pork Chop for helping us out."

"Man, you and Capp get a piece of chicken and a biscuit and eat."

"How much money do you have?"

"Man, I only have $5; by the way, I'm hungry, shit we *all* were hungry."

That was the best piece of chicken we ever had. After dropping Capp off to his dorm we headed back to North Carolina Central University; I arrived late. Needles to say, until this day, we never went back to give Pork Chop the money we promised him. Our intentions were good and we kept saying when we got more money we would go back and find Pork Chop but it never happened. I wonder what Pork Chop and that lady are doing today. I would love to see them again.

CHAPTER 30

Deciding My Major

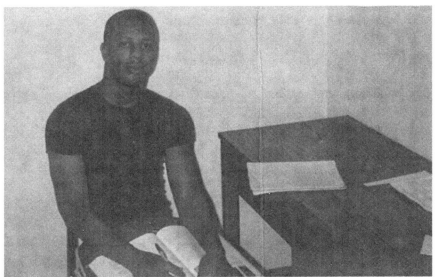
Me Studying During College Days

Finally decision time; it was put up or shut up! I had to make a decision at first I really didn't know what I wanted to go to school for, and what I wanted to do. I wasn't a bit more business minded than the man on the moon, I just said that because somebody else said that this was their major.

I remember earlier in my sophomore year I took Intro to Criminal Justice as an elective course and all of a sudden I was able to comprehend what I was reading. A clock went off in my head and I said, 'I like this.' The reason I liked criminal justice was because I was able to comprehend crime, because most of my friends was criminals. I was able to relate.

When the subject of probation and parole came up, I knew about this subject because the guys in Carver Courts that I used to swing with was going back and forth to jail and then they would get out on parole.

Criminal justice interests me because of the criminals I knew. I used to swing with the crooks until they go out and committed a crime. I had sense enough not to go but they would give me some of the items that they stole. I could have been locked up for receiving stolen goods. I knew this type of language, not through the books and Intro to Criminal Justice but growing up in Carver Courts.

Anyway that is how I got into Criminal Justice, that's when I started getting educated, started forming some type of idea of what I was going to do. My major was Political Science and Minor was Criminal Justice. On top of all of that pressure of deciding my major and getting my degree, my daughter Latoya was born and she was my responsibility.

Me and My Daughter, LaToya

I really started going home every week because I wanted to be more than a father, I wanted to be a man that stuck by his girlfriend during the pregnancy.

It is easy to get a woman pregnant but can you stand by the woman when she is actually carrying your baby, losing her shape, dealing with the mood swings.

I was the man for the job because of the way I was raised. It wasn't easy but I got through it and I made my grandmother proud because I was taking care of my responsibilities. I'm not saying my grandmother was happy I got someone pregnant being in college and without being married, I'm just saying that she witnessed the child she raised stepping up to the plate and handling his responsibilities.

Some men run from this responsibility but I embraced it. After LaToya was born, I said my party days were over with but not quite. Criminal Justice became easy to me so I didn't have to study as hard. I used to get in my blue 1965 Buick convertible. The boys and I used to go over to the University of North Carolina and party with that university.

Off to My Intern Job as an Adult Probation and Parole Officer

University of North Carolina was only twelve miles away from Durham, North Carolina. I used to see Michael Jordon all the time because that is where he went to school and he used to

come on the yard at North Carolina Central University to party with us. He would go straight to the student union to get his hair cut until he started wearing his head bald. I didn't know Jordan personally, and I'm not going to sit here and lie and say, 'Hey man I used to party with Michael Jordon and we were buddies." I didn't know Mike and he probably don't know me from Adam and Eve. We have spoken a couple of times in passing.

He was always a nice guy and I can honestly say I never saw Jordon with a beer in his hand, but I did see other athletes who eventually made it big in the professional leagues getting real wild at parties.

If Jordon were to see me today, he probably would say, 'This guy looks familiar, but I can't say that I know him.' Michael Jordon was always professional every time I seen him. When I tell people that we played against Michael Jordon, they don't believe me as if Michael Jordon just all of a sudden just drops out of the sky and played professional basketball.

First and foremost, Michael Jordon was born just like everyone else, he went to school just like everyone else, and he played sports. He is from Wilmington, North Carolina which is only one hour from Kinston, North Carolina, the place I where I grew up.

I used to have a homeboy that threw some wild parties in Chapel Hill, North Carolina; he had everything that most people wanted at parties, from beer to drugs. I used to see some famous athletes over there indulging but it was all good, at least they weren't fighting, but I can honestly say I never seen Jordon do anything illegally.

Whenever I drove my 1965 Buick Convertible over to the parties, I had another homeboy traveling with me; he was what I would call a male groupie he used to go over to the parties with his weed. He sold a little weed himself and would love to go around famous athletes and let them get their weed for free just to say he smoked weed with this athlete. These guys used to *use* Fred, and they loved riding in the convertible.

Those days are long gone...I am not trying to down any athlete or anything of that nature and I don't want to mention any names as to who was doing what, but what I will say is,

'Michael Jordan, was a the model athlete in North Carolina during my time era.'

CHAPTER 31

Getting in a Fight at the University of North Carolina

I was *still* partying in school; one particular night I went over to the University of North Carolina for a party and met Derrick Moore. He was a homeboy.

This football player that played with the University of North Carolina made a mistake and stepped on Moe's shoes and didn't apologize. I can't think of the guys name but he went on to play professional ball.

Moe asked the guy, "Do you wear the same size shoe that I wear?"

I guess the guy didn't understand what Moe was saying, hell, I didn't understand what Moe was saying. Moe always came out if his mouth with that D.C. slang.

The guy asked, "What are you talking about?"

"Motherfucka' you stepped on my shoes and didn't apologize!"

An argument began and got real heated. Most of the University of North Carolina football players came over to help their teammate out. It wasn't anybody but me, Moe, Poonie and my cousin Pooh who were at the party from Central. We couldn't fight the University of North Carolina Football team by ourselves. Those guys were big as hell.

When the whole football team, surrounded us I told Moe, "You need to chill; we are on their turf."

Moe had been drinking and didn't care. We got Moe out of the party and went back over to Central. Another time when Moe and I went to D.C., he advised me not to say anything to these Prince George County police nor these Fairfax County policemen, they will locked you up fast.

After going to a couple of Go-Go clubs and drinking, our tempers were bad. I think we went to a club called, *Chapter 3* first located in D.C. - a big fight broke out.

"Man, I'm ready to leave this club."

"Well let's go to the *Gold Room* to party. I think the group 'EU' or 'Rare Essence' was playing there that night and when those guys get on stage, they play for about five hours straight and the people dance for five hours straight. Washington D.C. created the Go-Go and the father of Go-Go is Chuck Brown.

After we left the club, Moe suggested that we go to I.H.O.P. (International House of Pancakes) to get something to eat. Moe got into an argument with the *same* policemen that he told me not to say anything to because of their reputation of beating you down.

I had to use the bathroom real bad so I went to the bushes to use the restroom. The policeman came over to arrest me for using the restroom outside. Moe stepped in between us and said, "Man, he wasn't doing anything but using the restroom."

I think the policeman told Moe to stay out of it; then the policeman and Moe got into an argument. I thought they were going to beat Moe down. After all, they did have a reputation of beating a brotha' down especially in Fairfax County. Those white policemen would beat you down and not think anything of it.

Eventually I apologized to the policemen and we went into I.H.O.P and ate until our high came down. I think we drank a little too much alcohol that night.

Every time I see Moe now, we talk about what happened. The next day we drove back to North Carolina and made it back in time for me to catch my 9 a.m. class; being that I didn't have any books I couldn't afford to miss any classes. I had another roommate named Little Jim and I'm glad he didn't make that trip to D.C. with us because when Jim goes to drinking, you know that it is going to be some mess, because Jim was never able to hold his alcohol. You either had to pray or get away from Jim when he is drinking. These were the only two options. The funny thing about Jim is that he couldn't remember anything the next morning.

CHAPTER 32

The Night 'Little Jim' Flipped

I haven't talked about Jim that much in this book, but boy he was something else. Jim was my roommate when I moved off campus. He was a homeboy that was about ten years older than me; he had a history in Kinston, the history was his drinking.

Jim was a very good person it's just that he turned into another person when he drank alcohol. Ten years before I got to North Carolina Central University, Jim had attended it as well, as did so many of the homeboys. Most of them dropped out and just stayed in Durham, North Carolina.

When I arrived and started to attend school, Jim said, "Man I can't believe you are in college already. I'm going back to finish up the couple of hours I had before I dropped out because I'm not going to let you get your degree before I get my degree, boy, I raised you."

All of the older people loved to say they raised me. I told Jim, "I'm looking forward to moving off campus."

"We can be roommates," he suggested.

"I'm down."

We got an apartment on Fayetteville Street called, Parkview Apartments. Jim and I got a two bedroom. We didn't have any furniture so I got my mother's couch, a recliner from storage and an old coffee table. I didn't have a bed; I slept on the couch or a sleeping bag.

Jim was working at the Durham County Library at the time. It just so happened that we lived only one door from where Jim and the Kinston crew had lived ten years earlier.

We had a lady named Sonya living in the apartment above; she was our mother away from home. She was staying in Parkview when Jim lived there ten years earlier. Our apartment was always packed; all of the home people used to come over. Sometimes you couldn't tell whether you were in Kinston or Durham. Weed was being sold out of that apartment. I wasn't into the weed but I was drinking Budweiser or either Private

Stock Beer; I have already mentioned the liquor I drank - Courvoisier.

I knew Jim was selling weed but he tried not to sell anything in front of me. He would always take his customers to the back or if I was in my room, he would take care of business in the living room. My attitude was, *'he could do whatever he wanted to do as long as I was not a part of it.'* He used to always say, "Gold if something happens to you, your Uncle Hamm told me he was going to kick my ass."

One time during homecoming, Jim got so tore up that when we left to go to the homecoming show, he said he would meet us there. We had visitors from out of town staying with us, any time anyone from Kinston came up to stay or visit, our spot was the spot they came to.

We had our tickets to see the O'Jays, Mtume and Chaka Khan. When the other homeboys and I went to the show, we left Jim at the house with a beer in his hand and a joint in his mouth. Chaka Khan was looking so good at the show, I told one of the homeboys, "I have to go back stage to meet her," especially when she broke out and started singing, '*Sweet Thing.*'

I proceeded to go to the back of the stage; I got through the first rope without being stopped. When I got to the second rope, security said, "You can't go backstage."

Antray was visiting at the time and told me, "Let's go back to our seats."

Antray and I had always been the best of friends. After the show, we went everywhere and to all the parties. We never did see Jim at the show. We thought maybe we didn't see him because it was so crowded and we'd missed him. We arrived back home about 5 a.m. I stuck my key in the door; Jim was laid out on the couch with his show ticket in his hands. He had passed out from drinking too much.

I will never forget another time when we had a homeboy to come and stay with us for about two weeks; his name was C-los. He sold weed back in Kinston.

One evening when Jim got off from work his income taxes was in the mail. The next day two more homeboys came by the house and said let's go out to a club. I forgot to mention when Jim got home he had a bottle of Hennessey. We all drank and as you know I couldn't smoke the weed.

Anyway, we decided to go to this new club in Raleigh, North Carolina named, *Taboos* owned by this big fat guy that played in all of those movies called, Training Academy. In the movie he was the biggest black fat guy with the police officer uniform on.

When we walked in the club Thad was at the door; we paid and went to the upstairs area. Our homeboy C-los thought we were in Kinston, he took out his weed and proceeded to roll a joint. We had to tell C-los that this was not *D&M Club* back in Kinston. This was a top notch club; he needed to put that away. Of course, all of us had been drinking before we got there, but Jim's *other personality* hadn't come out yet. It only came out when he drank beer and liquor. When the waitress came around to take our order of drinks, Jim said he was paying for all of our drinks.

It was just four of us and Jim was beginning to allow his second personality to come out but even with this, he knew how to count his money. I don't care how drunk he got; it was hard to cheat him. When the lady got back with the drinks, she started counting Jim back his money, when she was counting the money back to him, she told Jim that it was a *ten dollar bill*; she was really giving him a *one dollar bill*.

Jim knocked all the drinks off the tray and said, "B-, you trying to cheat me!"

That's when all hell broke loose. The bouncers came over and grabbed Jim; I told one of the bouncers, "Let me handle him."

"If you don't get control of him, we are throwing his ass out of the club."

I told Jim, "Calm down."

"I'm not calming down that b- tried to cheat me!"

One of the homeboys and I went downstairs to go dance and before we knew it, we looked upstairs and we could tell a lot of commotion was going on and then we saw Jim. We ran from off the dance floor to go get Jim.

When we got upstairs, the bouncers already had Jim in the air. Jim wore glasses and half of his glasses were hanging off of his face. I told the bouncer, "Let me take him home!"

"No, we are kicking him out!"

"I agree that he should be out of the club but let me take him out."

I knew they were getting ready to beat Jim's ass. One of the bouncers pushed me back.

"I'm not Jim; I am just as big as you are! If you put your hands on me again, me and you will be fighting! I am trying to bring peace by taking Jim out of the club."

As soon as the bouncers let Jim go and before I could grab Jim, he swung at them; all of the bouncers grabbed Jim and picked him up, took him down stairs and threw Jim on the gravel outside of the club. They told Jim that he couldn't come back in.

Jim said, "M- F- I will be back!"

I had forgotten about the fact that Jim carried his gun everywhere he went. Jim ran towards the car; I went back to get the homeboys and told them, "We are leaving."

As soon as we came back out of the club, Jim had his gun walking towards the club. Thank God that we came back out of the club when we did. If we didn't, Jim would have started shooting. We took the gun from Jim because we heard someone say, 'they called the police.' We put Jim in the car and hauled ass out of the parking lot and went back to Durham. I was so afraid because I just knew someone had taken our tag number and told the police.

When we arrived in Durham, we stopped by Hardees restaurant and ordered some food to take back to the apartment. I could tell Jim was still drunk because he had that glaze in his eyes. We ate our food and Jim went to bed. Me and the fellows stayed up a little while and talked about what had happened and then we went to bed. The next morning Jim didn't remember anything.

CHAPTER 33

God Was Warning Me

In the last two years of college there was too much going on in my life. Trouble was following me every where I went. When I returned to Kinston to visit and go to the clubs, someone would always pick a fight. I was never a person that started trouble but I didn't back down from anything. I had to take a step back and try to figure out what was going on. 'Was I hanging around the wrong crowd or was I at the wrong place at the wrong time.'

The friends I had weren't the fighting type, and they never started trouble either. I began to take notice of what was going on but I couldn't put my finger on it. I knew something bad was going to happen to me but I didn't know what. One night I had this dream that I was riding in my classic; this is what I called my 1965 Buick convertible...in my dream I wrecked my car and I dreamt that I was paralyzed and when it came to my college graduation, I wasn't able to walk across that stage.

This dream took place in the middle of all the troubles that I was running into which was out of character for me. There were so many troublesome incidents I encountered while I was in college that I can't tell them all, but an alarm should have went off in my head during this one incident.

By now Jim and I had another roommate which was another close friend of mine, basically just like a brother to me. Jim never really liked him but this brotha' would give you the shirt off of his back - he and Jim stayed in the same Parkview Apartments back in the 70's. Jim didn't want him to stay there but like I said before we all lived in Carver Courts together and our families were tight and plus he was a Jones.

Jim had made the comment to him, "The only reason you are staying here is because of Goldwater so let's get this straight, I don't want you here but Goldwater does. As long as you come up with your share of the money every month, this will not be a problem and you and Goldwater will be sharing rooms."

My friend Hook was free hearted, a little too free hearted at times. If a stranger walked by he would welcome the stranger in the house and invite him to our thin food and drinks. I remember walking in the house one day and this guy who I didn't know, was drinking a Budweiser. I didn't think anything of it; I just spoke and went on about my business. Later on when Jim got off from work he went in the refrigerator to get his beer and he said, "Gold, did you drink my beer."

Of course he didn't mind if I had drank the beer; he would just go out and buy another six-pack. He said, "I know Hook don't drink, so who drank my beer?"

Hook told Jim, "A friend came over so I offered him a beer."

"Don't offer nobody my shit, you can offer people *your stuff* in this house but don't you ever give anyone none of what belongs to me unless I said they could have it!"

The same thing would happen to me when I would come to the apartment and go in the closet and get my liquor and most of it was gone. The people in the neighborhood knew Hook was free hearted so they would continue to come around just to get high. One day I got a call from of one of my homeboys for me to pick him up from Raleigh/Durham Airport, like I said earlier our apartment is where everyone would stay if they were in town.

I used to pick up this guy named Little Wayne from the airport all the time, he may stay two or three days or he may stay a week, most of the times I would go to Kinston for the weekend so therefore I wasn't there that much. Little Wayne had just flown from New York to Raleigh/Durham. Every time I would pick him up he would fill my tank up, he was my father's age but he called himself raising me too.

One night Little Wayne and Hook were talking in the living room and it was getting late so I decided to go to bed. I woke up about an hour later and Hook and Little Wayne were still talking. I went to use the bathroom and when I came out I noticed their eyes were glossy and when I went into the kitchen, I saw this big ass scale that a person would see in the science class. I saw enough cocaine to get everyone in Durham high. I went on back to sleep.

I didn't say anything but I did think to myself, 'I know this guy isn't selling this shit and I know he didn't have this when I picked him up from the airport. I am more than sure he didn't have it with him.' Like I said before my homeboys will do their best not to let me see them do anything, smoking a joint, yes, but everything else, no.

I went back to sleep for another two hours and I remember someone coming in my room cutting on the light. It's hard for me to sleep with the light on. When I opened my eyes, they weren't fully focused but I did see Little Wayne with a gun and Hook telling Little Wayne everything was alright. Little Wayne had come in my room and turned over some clothes. I got up and wanted to know what the hell was going on and why Little Wayne was waving his gun around as if he was looking for something.

He was my homeboy so I wasn't worried about him shooting me. I walked in the living room and the furniture was turned over and all the cabinets were opened. Little Wayne said, "There were people in the house trying to kill us!"

It didn't take a genius to figure out that Little Wayne was hitting too much of his own stuff. Not only was he hitting too much of his own stuff, but he started having flashbacks of Vietnam. Little Wayne came in the living room and started shouting, "Everyone duck, there is the enemy!"

I didn't see any enemies, me, Hook, and Little Wayne were the only ones in the house.

I knew our neighbors heard what was going on especially Arthur and his brother next door; their last name was Jones also. As I mentioned earlier, when Jim and I moved in our apartment, Jim said, "Damn, the apartment next door is where we used to stay in the 70's."

Like I said earlier, I knew Little Wayne wasn't going to hurt us, but he kept seeing people in the house and I kept saying there isn't anyone in here and if they were, the closet was too little for them to hide in. It was hard to talk to Little Wayne with that gun waving around, he was a homeboy and we couldn't put him out because his brother back in Kinston would have thought we done him wrong. It was fifteen degrees that night.

I told Hook, "You can take the classic and take Little Wayne back to Kinston, just make it back before class tomorrow."

Little Wayne agreed that he would go back home. I remember Hook and Little Wayne getting in the classic to go back to Kinston; he still had the gun in his hand. I went back to the room and went back to sleep. Thirty minutes later, Hook came back to the house.

"I know you didn't go to Kinston and back that fast. Where is Little Wayne?"

"Gold, when we got by the research triangle area, Little Wayne made me get out of the car and open up the hood because he said someone was in there under the hood. He also made me open the glove compartment because he thought someone was there. Gold, the way Little Wayne was waving that gun around I was too damn nervous to drive."

It was ironic that Hook would use a curse word because I never heard him curse before.

"Well where is he?"

"I turned the car around and came back and when I got on Fayetteville street, Wayne told me to let him out."

"Hook, man we got to find him because it is freezing outside."

"Little Wayne was the one who wanted to get out of the car and walk."

An hour later, I saw a lot of lights outside our door. I peeked out the curtains and I seen a lot of police cars and the Swat Team going next door. I wanted to know, 'What in the world was the Swat Team doing at the home of Arthur and his brother. They didn't do anything but work on cars. They didn't even drink.'

After the Swat Team left, I heard a knock on my window and when I looked out, it was Little Wayne.

"Open the door!"

I opened the door and asked, "Are you alright?"

He said, "Yes."

I could tell he wasn't as high as he was before he left but he still had the gun. He said he wanted to apologize to me and Hook; we couldn't go back to sleep. Little Wayne asked Hook could he take him back to Kinston?

"You have to wait until I get out of class tomorrow."

The next day I saw Arthur and asked him why was the Swat Team at their house last night. He said someone had told the police that the Jones boys was being held hostage. Remember I said earlier that the guys who stayed next door were also Joneses.

"Give me more details," I said to Arthur.

He said, "The police knocked on the door and asked do the Jones boys stay here? I told them, 'Me and my brothers' last name are Jones.' Then the police asked me were we being held hostage and I told him, 'no,' but they said they had to check the apartment out anyway.

The police said that some short fellow stopped them last night and gave them their address and said the Jones boys were being held hostage."

I turned around and looked at Little Wayne and he had this fucked up look on his face. I asked little Wayne, "Did you send the police over to our neighbor's apartments?"

"Yes."

Little Wayne's mind had gone back to the 70's to the same apartment that they had lived in. Me and Hook were the Jones boys that Little Wayne told the police about. He gave them the apartment number of Arthur and that set of Joneses... I was so pissed off and glad at the same time because if the police would have come to me and Hook's apartment and asked where we being held hostage? We would have said no. When the police would have told us that they had to check the apartment out anyway they would have found enough cocaine to get everyone high in Durham and also a scale big enough to weigh an animal on.

We would have gone to jail for a long time for something we knew nothing about, let me take that back, I would have gone to jail for something I *didn't have anything to do with*. Even if Little Wayne and Hook would have taken the blame for what happened and told the police that I didn't have anything to do with the drugs, the police wouldn't believe them. I would have still been in prison now if this incident would have occurred. The police would have gotten me for <u>*conspiracy*</u> because the drugs were at the house.

"Take Little Wayne back to Kinston."

This wasn't the first time Little Wayne had done something like that. I remember when I wasn't in town for the weekend, Little Wayne had come from New York again but Hook picked him up from the airport. They started getting high and Little Wayne told Hook to *close the curtains because the police was in the trees*. Hook tried to convince him that no one was in the trees. Little Wayne got his gun and shot up in the ceiling and just so happen 'our mother away from home,' Sonya, was in the bathroom at the time and the bullet came up through the ceiling and went straight through her bathroom missing her by a couple of inches.

Sonya came down stairs to see what was going on; she and Hook had to convince Little Wayne that there wasn't any policemen in the trees. Sonya had a long talk with Little Wayne about him having to get himself together because things were getting out of hand with him. Sonya loved all of us from Kinston. Wayne promised that he would get himself together.

Little did I know that Wayne was going back and forth to New York to pick up drugs; I'm glad I didn't know because I would have been very uncomfortable around him. I still wasn't getting the message that God was trying to convey to me, he was warning me that something was going to happen but I just wasn't getting it. There were more things that happened before I got the message. It was too late because I suffered for not heeding God's warning.

CHAPTER 34

My Friend Ross Killed His Girlfriend

While attending North Carolina Central University, I met a friend named Ross; Ross had a blacker than midnight blue skin tone and his stature was like Arnold Schwarzenegger; he drove a Volvo and was quiet and cool. He never messed with anybody; there was a time that I thought he played with North Carolina Central University Football Team, but after talking with him, he told me that he wasn't on the team.

He told me he transferred from East Carolina University. I didn't know much about Ross but I do remember someone saying Ross had to sit out a semester because when he had gone home for spring break and while he was at a party one night, someone slipped something in his drink that made him do weird things.

When Ross got himself together, he came back to school. I

think this activity happened before I came to North Carolina Central University. I really can't say whether what they say happened to Ross is true or not but I am aware of people saying he used to be behind his apartment burning the Bible but nevertheless that was the story on Ross.

Around me he never *displayed* any of those rumors that I'd heard. He was one of the nicest guys I had ever met. One Monday evening, Ross and his girlfriend came by the apartment and asked for my roommate; my roommate was selling weed at the time. My roommate would be slick when he was selling this stuff; he didn't want me to see this because they knew my family and they knew my family wouldn't stand for that activity but what they did was their business.

Anyway when I came out of the room, I spoke to Ross and his girlfriend. Ross asked me, "What are you getting ready to do?"

"I have a class from 7 p.m. to 9:30 p.m."

"Come over to my apartment to see the game after class."

"I'll stop by."

I remember it as if it were yesterday, because Ross and I were Cowboy fans and the Cowboys were playing St. Louis Cardinals for Monday Night Football. Ross didn't drink but I told him I would bring a six pack of Budweiser over for the game.

At 8:45 p.m. I slipped out of class and went to the store to get the beer and headed to Ross's apartment, just as I was arriving at the place, it had been surrounded with detective cars, the Durham County police cars; there was this crime scene with the yellow tape.

I proceeded to go to the apartment with my beer; I remember saying to myself, '*That looks like Ross apartment.*'

The T.V. crew came over to me and asked, "Do you know this guy Ross?"

"Yes."

The police wanted to talk to me but the T.V. crew wanted to get their information first.

The T.V. crew asked me, "How do you know him?"

"Because he is a friend of mine; I came over to watch football." I wasn't looking directly in the camera while I was talking; my mind was on what happened. I remember the T.V. crew asking me, 'What type of guy was he?"

"He is a nice guy."

"Did he have a girlfriend?"

"Yes."

They were asking me all of those questions because there was a girl found behind the apartment with about forty stab wounds and they didn't know who she was. The police came over to talk with me because they didn't know whether or not I may have had something to do with the crime or whether I knew what went on. They were being slick with their questions and I was being truthful with my answers. The police still wouldn't tell me what happened and now when I think about it, they didn't want to give me any information just in case I was a possible aide in the crime.

One of the bystanders came over after the police had stop questioning me and said, "I heard someone hollering, so I came out of the apartment and seen Ross with no clothes on running from the apartment. Ross had stopped a lady at the traffic light and snatched her out of the car and took off down the highway. When the police stopped the car, he got out and I guess the police tried to rush him and he broke one of the policeman's collar bone and from what I seen on the news, he was on the trunk of the car with no clothes on and the police roped him as if he were a beast to get him under control."

Later in my life, after graduating from college and having started my career, I was working at Triangle Correctional Center in Raleigh, N.C., Ross was at Central Prison. For some strange reason when I found out Ross was doing time over at Central Prison, I sent word over by someone to ask Ross if he remembered me. They stated he'd said he did but just barely.

When Ross had awakened the morning after his arrest,

it was my understanding that he could not remember committing the murder.

I often wonder, if I could have prevented what happened if I had gotten out of class a little earlier, or would *I* have been Ross's victim or would Ross have been *my* victim.

Was this another warning from God? Was God still trying to speak to me? These are questions that will linger in my mind and remain in the back of my mind for the rest of my life. Was God trying to save me?

Though I don't know where Ross is at this time, I am hoping that God has given Val's family the peace to close this painful chapter of their lives.

CHAPTER 35

God's Warning Came to Fruition

Earlier I mentioned that I had a dream that I was in a terrible car accident. I dreamed that I had gotten in a car accident in that blue convertible. I was laid up in the hospital paralyzed. The only thing that went on in my mind is the fact that I wasn't going to march with my class. I only had a few more weeks to my college graduation.

During the week of March 09, 1986, my college was out for spring break, this was my last year of college. I was scheduled to graduate on time, (meaning the four years). When I arrived in Kinston, North Carolina, I went to spend time with my girlfriend and my daughter who was nine months old. I kept her during that week because my girlfriend was also attending college. She attended Lenoir Community College.

A couple of days after I came home for spring break, I got sick and went to the emergency room because I had a high fever and I had the chills. The doctors diagnosed me with having a stomach virus. I got better as the week went by. My friend Capp was also home on spring break from Fayetteville State University. Another one of my friends was home from Germany because his father had passed away.

It had been a long time since me, Todd and Capp and the rest of the crew was home all at the same time. The fellows and I went to the barber shop that day to get a haircut. One of my friends that were in the barber shop cutting hair asked if we were going to the *Chic Disco Tech* later on that night. The Chic was a popular disco tech in my hometown. For the previous nine weeks the Chic was giving away a $100 for the talent show contest and the winner advanced to the final round.

This particular weekend the Chic was going to pick the winner for the final contest and give away a thousand dollars. My friend who was a barber was in the contest and everyone felt like he was going to win. While me and the fellows were at the barber shop he asked us to come out and cheer for him and the fellows said, 'Sure, we're coming.'

I knew I hadn't spent a lot of time with my girlfriend and daughter during spring break so I was trying to figure out how was I'm going to tell my girlfriend that I was going out with the fellows that night. After leaving the barber shop, we told each other that we will get up with each other later on. I went to my grandmother's house and started watching basketball, it was March Madness and I think it was the final four weekend.

Later on I went over to my girlfriend's apartment to spend some time with them. Guilt came over me about going out to party that night because I knew I hadn't spent time with my girlfriend, her son and my daughter. Something inside of me was saying, 'Don't go,' and, 'If the fellows don't call, don't you call them'; but also at the same time, my mind was saying, 'Man, you are getting ready to graduate in seven more weeks and then you will be able to spend all the time you want to with your girl and children.'

Todd called and said, "I will be coming to pick you up around 10 p.m." I told my girlfriend that I was going out for about two hours. I knew I had to leave to go back to college the next day. When Todd arrived to pick me up, I had that look on my face and the guilt in my heart about going out knowing that I hadn't spent time with the family.

Todd and I arrived at Capp's and he said he wasn't ready and he would meet us at the club later on. We called Antray and he said he would meet us at the club. When Todd and I arrived at the club and went inside, my cousin Eric came over and asked me what I was drinking. I think I told him to go get me a private stock beer. J.T. came over and asked me what time was I leaving to go back Sunday and could he catch a ride back to school. I told him, 'Yes.'

Todd, his girlfriend and I were standing around chilling and waiting for the crew to get to the club. The D.J. announced that the talent competition would be starting in ten minutes, so most of the crowd started heading to the front of the stage...I remember Todd, his girlfriend and I started heading to the stage. Some guy came out of no where and put his hands on Todd girlfriend's ass.

Todd and the guy got into an argument and I got between them and told Todd to drop the shit. The guy Todd was arguing with told me to stay out of it and told me if I wanted to *I* could get some of the action. As a matter of fact, the guy invited me outside to fight.

"I'm not going outside; if I was going to fight you it would be right now."

The guy kept on trying to get me to leave the club but I refused. For some reason, I didn't feel like fighting that night and plus I was dressed with a nice sport jacket on as well as a pair of slacks and my Pierre Cardin leather boots. I was too clean.

The guy called me a punk ass motherfucker because I wouldn't go outside. I couldn't believe I was taking this kind of verbal abuse because any other time if someone had disrespected me, it would have been on.

After the guy couldn't convince me to go outside, I proceeded to get closer to the stage to watch the talent show. Five minutes later someone hit me in the back of the head with their fist and when I turned around, it was the same guy who I had an argument with a few minutes earlier.

I hit the guy about five times with my fist and then I picked him up over my head and body slammed him on the table and commenced to whipping his ass. He managed to bust my lip while he was on the ground and that's when I put both of my knees on each one of his arms where he couldn't swing anymore. I just started beating the hell out of the guy. The next thing I knew someone was pulling me up off the guy and handing *him* a gun at the same time.

At first I didn't see the gun until he pointed the gun in my face and shot the gun twice but the gun misfired. I was able to turn and that's when I felt something hitting me in my right bottom hip in the butt area and all of a sudden my whole right side became numb.

I was trying to get away and that's when the guy shot me on the left hip below my butt; all of a sudden, I couldn't feel my left nor my right leg. That's when I fell to the floor. The guy stood over me and shot towards my face but he missed and the gun jammed.

While I was lying on the floor, Antray came over and said, "Man let's go! Someone has started shooting up in here!"

"I'm the one who got shot."

"Stop playing. We got to go!"

I kept telling him, "I'm the one who has been shot."

Antray wasn't convinced, so I had to pull my pants down a little to show him the blood. I could tell I was going into shock because I started getting the 'cotton mouth.'

My cousin Eric came over with the beer that he said he was getting for me earlier when I first came to the club. I hadn't been in that club twenty minutes before all of this drama took place.

"Give me the beer because I can feel my throat closing in on me," it was to the point that I was about to choke, "call the ambulance!"

One of the workers at the club said they had already called the ambulance.

"Call them again, because the ambulance is taking too long"... I told the fellows, "I can't feel anything from the waist down and they needed to pick me up to take me to the car;" I drank the beer first.

When the fellows picked me up and put me inside the car, I remembered the top part of my body feeling cold.

"What are you waiting for," I asked Antray.

"I am waiting for the car to warm up and plus I can't go anywhere because another car has us blocked in."

Then all of a sudden I heard another gunshot go off.

I asked the guys to cover me, "I think this fool is coming back to finish me off," but he had already left the scene; the shot I heard was someone else shooting in the air.

"We need to go; I need to get some medical attention. Back the car up and ride on the sidewalk and get me the hell out of here!"

When we were on our way to the hospital, we passed the ambulance. After arriving at the hospital, the fellows took me out of the car and took me inside the hospital. I saw a lot of people that was in the club at the hospital. I seen my cousin Sharon Mason crying.

The fellows asked the nurse to get a gurney to put me on; the nurse that was working asked, "Aren't you the same guy that was in here Monday with a stomach virus," she said, "What were you doing out in the streets?"

When the nurse wheeled me back where the doctors cared for you, my cousin Eric was acting like a pure fool, he kept saying, 'I'm going to kill the motherfucker that shot my cousin!'

The nurse told him that he had to leave the area that I was in or she would have to call the police. Eric refused to leave and the police came and arrested him. The crowd was getting loud at the hospital. The nurse asked another one of my friends named Albert to leave the area and he refused to leave. He said he wasn't going anywhere until my grandmother came.

Albert was a big weightlifting guy and the police didn't bother him. Word had started spreading that I had gotten shot and more people were coming to the hospital...things were getting out of hand. The nurse started hooking me up to the I.V. and one nurse came over and just shoved a tube down my nose and I snatched the tube out because I was choking. This nurse didn't have any tack.

Another nurse came over and said, "Garry, you are bleeding inside of your stomach and we have to put this tube down your throat"...she said, "I'm going to take my time and as I push the tube down your nose, I want you to swallow and this will make the procedure easier."

The procedure was easier with the second nurse; the first nurse who was white treated me like shit. On top of that, the doctor came in and asked in a sarcastic manner, "What were you doing at the bar?"

"I wasn't at no damn bar...you're going to talk to me like you got some sense."

He said, "I don't like to be called late at night."

After he had made this statement, I could have busted that joker in the head. I guess he felt like I made his job hard; he was frustrated because he was a specialist and had to be called in the middle of the night. The doctor told the nurse to put this long needle in my penis and I asked what in the hell are you all going to do with me. By this time my grandmother had arrived at the hospital. When the nurse tried to put the needle down my penis, I started hollering and cursing, my grandmother told me that I better shut that fuss and I better not curse again.

If the doctor would have told me what was going on, it would have been much better. They were prepping me for surgery and they were hooking a colostomy bag up to me because they had seen a lot of blood in my stomach. My girlfriend walked in the hospital and the first thing I asked her, "Who is home with the children?"

She told me her mother came to the apartment to stay with them. She was trying to convince me that everything was going to be alright. I wasn't buying this shit. I couldn't feel anything from waist down, and I was being hooked up to a colostomy bag. They thought the bullet might have hit my kidneys.

I kept saying, 'I'm going to kill that guy who shot me!' My Uncle Jay kept telling me that I couldn't say that because if something happened to the guy who shot me, they are going to charge me with a crime - conspiracy.

The doctor said again, "You didn't have any business at no bar; I can smell alcohol on your breath."

"I had a beer because after I had been shot my mouth got dry."

The hospital staff wheeled me to the operating room to do exploratory surgery.

"Am I going to be paralyzed?"

"I don't know," the doctor said.

"Will I have to wear this colostomy bag for the rest of my life?"

"I don't know."

It appeared to me that the doctors didn't know a damn thing. I awakened the next morning in a regular room. I.V.'s were running every where, tubes down my nose. I was in a complete mess, not knowing whether or not I would walk again.

All of these nurses kept coming in with all this green on, I was trying to figure out what was going on, someone told me it was Saint's Patrick Day.

The police was in my room asking questions about what happen; I couldn't give them much detail.

"Did ya'll catch the guy?"

"No, but we know who he is because he shot two more people in the past."

The police said, "We spoke with the guy's friend that shot you; he told us that everything was a setup and that you didn't start the fight. He told us that him and his buddy tried to get you to go outside with them but, when you didn't go, his buddy told him to hold the gun because he was going back inside to get you and to only give him the gun if he was getting his ass kicked."

I guess if I would have lost the fight I would have never been shot. I suffered a long time after being shot and I still suffer today because during the summertime, my whole right side burns and during the winter time my right side aches. The bullet messed up my sciatic nerve. The good thing about it was that I wasn't paralyzed and a week later, the colostomy bag was taken out and I was able to use the bathroom on my on! I am so glad!

That ordeal was an eye opener! You see, when that gun didn't go off twice as the guy was looking down at me and I was looking up at him, I knew without a shadow of a doubt that there is a God and I know that he looks out for fools and babies. I wasn't either one of those that night, but I can honestly say that he is a Good God and I am grateful to be alive and well.

I think everybody that night was in rare form after the incident; Eric going to jail for being too concerned for his cousin or either the alcohol had gotten the best of him; Albert protecting me and the surroundings until my grandmother came or was it part of the drama, my getting shot and everything happened next as in, "*As the World Turns.*"

I went to Duke University Hospital to get operated on to remove the bullet and had several minor operations to ease the pain.

While in the hospital I was doing my work to graduate. One of my classmates would come by the room to retrieve my term paper and turn it in. She took my work to one of my drama classes and slid the paper under the door but the teacher had already went to the registrar office and turned in the grades and he never went back to his classroom. He didn't receive my term paper so he gave me an "I" - incomplete.

I didn't need this class to graduate, it was just an elective, but I couldn't get my diploma with an "I" on my grade. The university tried to track the teacher down because they wanted to see me march because I had come so far but they weren't able to reach the teacher until Monday - graduation was on that Saturday. When they reached the teacher and he saw my term paper he gave me a B. I picked up my diploma a few days later. The dream I had had earlier came true, I wasn't able to march with my class but I wasn't paralyzed.

God was trying to get my attention and I knew it but I didn't know what to do. What could I have done?

CHAPTER 36

No Justice No Peace

After I came back from Durham, North Carolina my mindset was to get justice for the person who shot me. I was still in a lot of pain because of permanent nerve damage so I decided to go back home and stay with my grandmother instead of my girlfriend's house.

My daughter was ten months old and she used to cry a lot and this was getting on my nerves. I needed peace of mind and because I was in so much pain I didn't need to be around anyone that I cared about because I was snappy.

My grandmother had patience, she could deal with my mood swings. I was in so much pain everyday that drinking alcohol was not taking care of the pain and the doctors took me off narcotics before I became hooked. I was told I will be in this condition for along time. I almost lost my damn mind. One minute my hold right side from waist down was burning and the next hour my whole right side from waist down was throbbing from so much pain. I was so desperate that I went to church and let the preacher put his hand on my leg to relieve the pain.

My friends used to come over to take me out of the house to get some air. One day I told them that they can take my car and let the convertible back and drive me around because I was walking with a cane.

After Being Shot Having to Walk With Cane

It was the 4th of July and everyone was out riding around or grilling. I was in the backseat of my car with my friend Antray and a fifth of Jim Bean.

"Pull over to the convenient store, because I want a cold beer," I said.

As Todd was pulling over to the store, Todd saw the guy that shot me. I didn't know what he looked like because when we fought that night in the club it was dark.

"Todd, are you sure that's him?"

"You damn right I'm sure!"

Antray confirmed this was the guy that shot me.

I said, "Let's get his ass, you all get out and catch him and bring him to me because I can't run!"

When the guy recognized that I was in the car, he took off running.

"Chase him in my car! Drive on the sidewalk if you have to!"

While Antray was chasing him, the guy ran through some projects and got away. I was pissed because I wanted revenge. The police and the trial were taking too long. He wasn't going to walk around Kinston after shooting me and think that he was going to get away with hurting me. After he shot the other two guys he walked around as though he couldn't be touched but I wasn't going to allow him to walk in peace. I wanted to send the message that, *'Every time you see me, you are going to run and eventually we are going to meet and I am going to beat the hell out of you the same way I beat you that night.'*

There was another occasion when my friends came over to the house to take me riding and we ended up at Southeast Park. The crowd would hang at Southeast for a few hours then they would go over to Holloway Park to hang out on Sundays.

I sat in the car for a few minutes because so many people were coming over to me to ask how I was doing.

One guy came over to me and said, "There is the guy that shot you, do you want me to take care of him."

"No, I want to do it myself. You can go ahead and put your gun up; I want to take care of him man to man."

The guy recognized my car this time and he took off to Holloway Courts. Eventually me and my boys headed to Holloway Courts and when I seen him, I hollered at him from a distance and told him, "Don't run!"

He pulled his gun out as if to say, 'if you come over I will shoot you again,' then he took off running. That's what cowards do, they don't fight with their hands; they want to use a gun. I grew up fighting with my hands.

One of my friends Albert was in the club one night and seen this guy again; Albert knew the guy because they were both stationed at Camp Lejeune Marine base together in Jacksonville, North Carolina. The guy seen Albert staring at him and went to tell the owner of the club that Albert was trying to start some trouble.

Albert wasn't trying to start any trouble but he was sending the guy a message that, *'you can not walk around Kinston at peace after shooting one of my friends and think you are going to get away with it so you might as well get used to getting your ass kicked whenever you are in public.'*

The owner of the club called the police and the guy left because Albert wasn't going anywhere. Albert was a body builder and he was strong as an ox, he didn't use a gun to fight anyone, he usually destroyed a person with his bare hands and if Albert Witherspoon or another friend of mines named Ike Bell say that they were going to get you, you might as well count on it. As a matter of fact you might as well go ahead and fight those two guys and get it over with because they will track you down until they find you.

This is ironic because Ike-B was the one who stabbed Albert back in the days when we were growing up in Carver Courts.

The next week it was time for me to go to trial and face the guy who shot me. The charges he was facing were assault with a deadly weapon, with intent to kill and inflicting serious bodily injuries. When we arrived in court the guy never showed up. A warrant was issued for his arrest but I received information that the guy went to his job to pick up his paycheck the week before he was scheduled for trial and never showed up for work anymore, he skipped town and went back to New York. I received No Justice and he is definitely not receiving No Peace.

It has been twenty-three years and the police still haven't caught this guy. Will they ever catch him, have they closed the case, is the guy dead, I don't know. The only thing I do know is that two thoughts enter my mind all the time and the thoughts are, 'Will I forgive the guy or will I get revenge?' I will never know the answer to this question until I face the guy who shot me.

EPILOGUE

Growing up when I used to hear people making the statement, "People are a product of their own environment," it was used in a negative connotation, but as I got older, I understood that we all are products of our environment whether it be positive or negative. I saw more positive growing up in Carver Courts so therefore I chose to follow the positive image that I seen and got from my family and the community. My last year in college during my spring break, I received two gun shot wounds stemming from an altercation that was about to happen and I stepped in to quell the situation. Ultimately a fight pursued, the tides turned and I became a victim. This incident never deterred me from making a positive impact in other people lives. The fact that I received two gun shot wounds, most people would have thought because I grew up in a housing project named Carver Courts that I was a product of my own environment which most people thought was negative. I don't condone violence nor do I glorify it, but reality is, it is what it is.

WHERE ARE THEY NOW

Front Row Left to Right, Uncle John Jones, Grandmother Tessie Jones and Uncle Earl Jones
Second Row Left to Right, Cousin Annie Mae Grimes, Aunt Mamie Johnson, Denderant Jones, Aunt Arnetta Dixon, Mother Vergie Chalmers, Aunt Mary Mason, and Aunt Mavis Jones

John Wesley Jones: Retired Principal from Lenoir County Public Schools - 36 Years

Tessie Simmons Jones: Domestic Work (Deceased)

Earl Kenlaw Jones: 25 Years at Manufacturing Plant (Deceased)

Annie Grimes Burt: 28 Years of Government Services to Present

Mamie Jones Johnson: Retired from Government Services 37 Years

Denderant Jones Burney: 30 Plus Years with Educational System to the Present

Arnetta Jones Dixon: 37 Years of Government Services (Deceased)

ARNETTA LOUISE DIXON

Vergie Jones Chalmers: 20 Years of Government Services

Mary Jones Mason: Retired from Government Services 30 Plus Years

Mavis Colleen Jones: 32 Years of Government Services to Present

First Row, Left to Right, Pete, Sharon, Tessie
Second Row, Left to Right, Lisa, Me (Mr. Cool) and Annie Mae

Left to Right Pete, Lisa, and of Course Me

My Grandmother, Tessie Jones and Me When I Was a Little Boy

My Grandfather, Wesley Jones

MY FATHER'S SIDE OF THE FAMILY

First Row: My Grandmother Frances Dove & My Grandfather Milton Dove Sr.
Second Row: My Aunt Timber Washington, My Aunt Kaye Jackson, My Aunt Lorna Dove, My Aunt Velma Dove & My Father Milton Dove Jr.

My Father Now

Left to Right: My Brother Duane King,
My Father Milton Dove Jr., My Sister Kayla Dove & My Sister Alicia Rooks

DEDICATION TO MICHAEL JACKSON

At 2:00 a.m. on October 28, 2009 I was reading about the documentary of Michael Jackson and how this was going to be his best performance ever!!! They said he looked good and he was dancing like he did 20 years ago.

In this country a person is supposed to be innocent until proven guilty; this was not the case with Michael Jackson along with so many others. Though Michael Jackson was proven innocent on all charges of child molestation, the same people who took him to the top were the same people who destroyed him – the media. Michael wasn't welcome by many in his own country, nor was Jesus.

After reading the comments of the documentary, I realized God allowed Michael Jackson to go out on top. Sometimes God will allow a person to die in order for the world to see what they have destroyed like when they destroyed his son Jesus.

After Jesus was executed, the Jews realized they killed the wrong person. After seeing the documentary on Jackson, some people are regretting what they did and the negative things they said about Michael. They said he was washed up, he couldn't do it anymore, he was weird and he was a freak. Take a look at the documentary and you tell me whether this man was washed up! He was the best damn performer the world has seen, including Elvis!

Me (in 2003), on the Hollywood Walk of Fame, Touching Michael Jackson's Star

CPSIA information can be obtained at www.ICGtesting.com
Printed in the USA
BVOW040559240812

298584BV00007B/37/P